# Home and Away

## OTHER BOOKS BY JAMES ORAM

*Neighbours: Behind the Scenes*
*Hogan: The Story of a Son of Oz*
(published in the US as
*G'Day America: The Paul Hogan Story)*
*The People's Pope*
*The Business of Pop*
*The Hellraisers* (with Jim Fagan)

## ABOUT THE AUTHOR

James Oram, a columnist and special writer for the *Sunday Telegraph,*
Sydney, has spent twenty years covering Australia, the South Pacific
and South-East Asia. His assignments have ranged from wars to royal
tours, from army coups to papal tours. This is his sixth book – his most
recent being the bestselling *Neighbours: Behind the Scenes.*

# Home and Away

## BEHIND THE SCENES

## JAMES ORAM

ANGUS
& ROBERTSON
PUBLISHERS

*ANGUS & ROBERTSON PUBLISHERS*

*16 Golden Square, London W1R 4BN,*
*United Kingdom, and*
*Unit 4, Eden Park, 31 Waterloo Road,*
*North Ryde, NSW, Australia 2113*

*First published in the United Kingdom by*
*Angus & Robertson (UK) in 1989*
*First published in Australia by*
*Angus & Robertson Publishers in 1989*

*Copyright © James Oram 1989*

*All black and white photographs copyright*
*© Solo Syndication 1989; colour*
*photographs copyright © Southdown*
*Press/Solo Syndication 1989*

*Typeset in Great Britain by*
*New Faces, Bedford*

*Printed in Great Britain by*
*Scotprint Ltd, Musselburgh, Scotland*

*British Library Cataloguing in Publication Data*

*Oram, James*
  *Home and away; behind the scenes*
  *1. Television drama series in English*
  *Home and away*
  *I. Title*
  *791.45'72*

*ISBN 0 207 16315 4*

# Contents

# 1

## How it all Began

The name of the town doesn't matter. It lies in southern New South Wales, scattered among other country towns with names that rollick on the tongue like Wagga Wagga, Cootamundra, Booroorban and Yarrawonga. There is one main street with shops, there are farm equipment suppliers, banks stuffed with mortgages, pubs, a couple of clubs and a park with a band rotunda. A river, dry for most of the year, cuts the town in half. Apart from droughts, floods, dust storms, hail storms, bush fires, grasshopper plagues and losses by the local football team, nothing much happened in the town and surrounding countryside to stir the community. Nothing much until work began on a building in the main street.

People looked at the building and swore. Farmers walked past it and cursed. Shopkeepers spoke angrily about it to their customers and the customers gathered on street corners and uttered threats. Ratepayers wrote to the council about it and Worried Mother of Three wrote to the local newspaper. The building was not wanted in the country town.

During the arguments, the threats, the protests, the controversy, all of which were unknown outside the tight confines of the community, a Sydney television producer by the name of Alan Bateman drove into the town. The only reason he stopped was the heat. He wanted an ice cream.

A couple of locals were in the shop when he went to the counter. Waiting for his ice cream, he exchanged a few pleasantries with the locals and after discussing the weather, the most popular and often the only subject for conversation in a country town, he mentioned the new building going up across the street.

'The construction work, looks like business is good around here,' he said politely.

There was silence. Then someone grunted and someone muttered. And the ice cream was a long time coming.

'What's it going to be?' Bateman pressed on, unaware he was treading on the town's sore toe.

A local cleared his throat. 'What's it gonna be? I'll tell you what it's gonna be. A place for druggies, thieves and bludgers.'

The other local added, 'And prostitutes and poofters.'

'The scum of Sydney, it'll all be here,' said the shopkeeper. 'It won't be safe to go out after dark, you mark my words.'

'A jail?' asked Bateman, thinking it could be the only place to house such a remarkable collection of deviants.

'Nah, one of those bloody homes for foster kids. Kids from the city. No right bringing 'em here.'

By the time he got his ice cream Bateman was aware that a plan to house foster kids in the country town had divided the community, had caused trouble and strife unheard of since the last rate increase. The town saw the foster home as nothing more than a scheme to import all the problems of the city into their relatively quiet way of life.

Returning to his car, he digested both his ice cream and what he had heard. And had he been a cartoon character a light bulb would have lit up above his head at that moment.

'I saw then the outline for a serial,' Bateman said. 'I had wanted to make a serial but I hate copycat television. I wanted to do something that really reflected the hopes, fears, challenges and ambience of young people in the 1980s. I believe young people are alienated to a certain extent nowadays. It is very tough growing up. They have to cope with unemployment and the family unit is a changing structure. Television shows were being written by middle-class, middle-aged people about what life used to be like, not what's happening in the Eighties. Then in the country town I saw it. Nobody in the community wanted them to move in and I began to wonder how streetwise city kids would adapt to the new lifestyle. Suddenly I thought, there is my slice of life in a community.'

Bateman knew what he was about. He had been in the business for thirty years, much of it with the Australian Broadcasting Commission, the Down Under equivalent of the BBC, where he rose to the not unimportant position of controller of television. Now he was director of drama for the Seven Network, which had its own stations in Sydney, Melbourne, Brisbane and Adelaide and affiliate stations throughout the country. He had notched up a few notable successes for the network, including 'Rafferty's Rules', a drama about a magistrate in a suburban court and the mini-series, 'Nancy Wake', about an Australian Second World War heroine. But the network badly wanted a daily soap opera. It once had one and it was called 'Neighbours'.

Back in 1985 the citizens of Ramsay Street belonged to the Seven Network, which had outlayed $A8 million to produce the five-times-a-week soap. The network was optimistic it had a hit on its hands but as the months passed a feeling came upon the executive corridors that 'Neighbours' was a turkey. Although it was doing well in Melbourne and reasonably in Brisbane, 'Neighbours' could not crack the country's biggest market in Sydney. After 171 episodes it was cancelled.

But the Grundy Organisation, producers of the soap, weren't so pessimistic and sold it to Network Ten, where it became a spectacular success before going on to do the sort of business in Britain television producers fantasise about. What happened to 'Neighbours' still causes nightmares among Seven Network executives. 'It hurts like hell,' confessed Glen Kinging, the programme director for Channel Seven, Sydney.

The network wasn't going to make the same mistake twice. No way. So Alan Bateman began working on the idea he got when he stopped to buy an ice cream in a country town. He returned several times to the town, keeping ears and eyes open as he chatted to the locals about the foster home and tried to understand their reactions but without letting on that beneath their noses a soapie was developing.

'I've never revealed the name of the town for the simple reason it was such a divided community,' said Bateman. 'I didn't want to stir up further antagonism. But what could be clearly seen was the conflict in the town. Some residents were violently opposed to what they saw as troublesome kids being dumped on their own doorstep. Others wanted to give them a go. It had all the elements of fine drama. You could bring a family together with many varied backgrounds – a family that is then thrown into a new environment where the problems of a group of streetwise kids come face to face with the traditional values of a small town on the edge of the urban sprawl.'

With a team of writers around him, he began extensive research into case histories of foster children, the unwanted, the abused, the lost and lonely kids who could not get along with their own parents but who, beneath their often tough exteriors, needed help and love as much as anyone, if not more so. Some were kids whose parents were both dead and who had been shunted from pillar to post, wanted by no one, and with each move their bitterness turned to anger, then rebellion. The furthest they were likely to get in life was head sweeper at the nearest jail. And yet they were only kids.

'Home and Away' was on the move.

The basic storyline was fleshed out. According to an early release from the Seven Network, it went this way: 'Tom and Pippa Fletcher were told they would never have children. They proved the experts wrong. But their family *is* different. The Fletcher kids come from broken homes, orphanages and institutions. Tom and Pippa take pot luck – they can never turn anyone away. But the family is plunged into financial crisis when Tom is retrenched from his job in the city. To forestall the government department's intention of removing the children, Tom and Pippa sell up and buy a rundown caravan park in a tiny coastal town called Summer Bay.'

Setting the location on the coast was a smart move. Australians love the coast, or more especially the endless beaches of white sand that circle the continent. Beaches are as much a part of life to the average Australian youngster, and most oldsters, as the mountains are to the Swiss, the deserts to the Arabs, lakes to the Canadians. They were taken to the beaches as toddlers, could surf well before they reached high school. Even in the far suburbs of a large city like Sydney the beach is never more than an hour away by train. And summer lasts forever.

The Australian Sunday is spent on the beach. Australians worship the many gods of sun and water and the beach is their temple. So devout are Australians in their worship they have established a tradition of spending Christmas Day on the beach in preference to dinner at home with turkey and plum pudding, perhaps to pray they will not get skin cancer, now recognised as a serious health problem.

Alas, beaches, or at least those strung along Sydney, once considered the finest in the world, are no longer the idyllic places portrayed in 'Home and Away'. There is nothing like Summer Bay left near Sydney. Political indifference has allowed the waters to become so polluted with sewage and chemicals that many people will put not as much as a toe into the sea. Some swimmers have picked up diseases and infections. Lifesavers are reluctant to bound into the surf. Beaches are frequently closed because of the sludge in the water.

Even the simple pleasure of lying on the sand, of basking like seals on a rock, has changed, as Australian writer, Gerard Lee, reported in the summer of 1988-89. 'Bondi Beach was like a huge public bed. People behaved as if they were at home in the privacy of their own boudoir. They'd lie about oblivious, cuddled up, topless, spooning, eating, reading, muttering. They were all in bed. Some of them would even lie on top of each other. I dare say some have done the whole thing. ... The beach was a leveller, but to me it was also a mind blower. I don't mind saying this, I was threatened ...'

But in spite of their destruction, beaches still remain an important part of the Australian culture. It was not always so. In the early 1900s Australians were barred from splashing in the ocean by restrictive laws which said it was illegal to bathe in the sea within view of other members of the public, that is near dwellings, bridges and streets, between the hours of 6am and 8pm. The puritanical authorities had the notion – and their notions were, incidentally, imported directly from Victorian Britain – that the sight of a person not clad from neck to toe, showing a knee here, an elbow there, would drive the population into an uncontrollable frenzy of lust. As no one wanted to go swimming in the dark, there being hungry sharks and treacherous currents beyond the surf line, the laws were largely ignored. But the authorities still pressed on with prosecutions, overstepping their mark when they felt the dog collar of the

*'Home and Away' was always destined to have a seaside setting –
here early members of the cast dangle their feet at 'Summer Bay'.
Left to right: Helena Bozich (Lynn), Kate Ritchie (Sally) and
Sharyn Hodgson (Carly)*

rector of St Mary's of Waverley, near Bondi Beach. The rector enjoyed a dip and his friends were incensed he should be prosecuted for participating in a harmless activity. They formed a group to help the clergyman in his legal battle. Out of the group came the first Australian lifesaving club, formed in 1906, and from then on the beaches were for everyone. They could swim when they liked. Now on a hot day there'll be 30,000 people on Bondi Beach, many of the women leaving the top part of their bikini at home.

Beaches became part of the Australian folklore. Tales were told of heroic rescues by lifesavers, books were written about sand and surf, movies were made on the subject. Going to the beach is as commonplace as strolling to the corner shop.

Yet, oddly, the beach had never been popularised before in a soap. 'Neighbours' was set in a suburban street, furthermore a suburban street in Melbourne where the closest beaches are poor things like Blackpool on a bad day. The denizens of Ramsay Street, it should be noted, spend their time in and around swimming pools, not on beaches. Another popular Australian soap, 'A Country Practice', is located in the country, as its name suggests. 'The Flying Doctors' is set in the harsh outback and an earlier favourite, 'Prisoner', remained behind the grim walls of a women's pokey. 'The Young Doctors', one of the longest-running soaps in Australia, was set in a hospital, easily the most popular location for a soap because doctors are considered heroic figures even when they put up their fees.

Not only would the beach allow a teenage audience to identify closely with the leisure activities of the younger members of the cast, it also meant that for any scenes only bathing costumes were needed. This allowed the cast to be displayed close to the way nature intended without offending the censors. It was also of considerable financial help to the wardrobe department.

Bateman was aware the soap had to feature characters the public, or at least the Australian public, would consider average. The Australian public was interested in Dallas-type serials only if they came from the United States, an expensive lesson learned when one channel launched a local serial called 'Taurus Rising' about Australian rich people, luxury mansions, expensive cars and helicopters. It went over like the proverbial lead balloon.

Bateman had the outline. Now he wanted to know the public's views on 'Home and Away', difficult because at the time he had nothing on film. He had only the broadest of stories, some characters, still pictures he made into slides and a brain brimming with ideas.

'Let's do it,' he said. 'Let's test what we've got on an audience.'

Coaxing a randomly selected audience into a Sydney auditorium, he gave what, after all, was little more than a slide show, the sort of thing once popular with returning missionaries at Sunday School. The audience liked it. The audience, in fact, thought it one of the better ideas seen in a long time. Bateman gave the green light for a pilot episode.

There were problems, as always when making pilots. Sometimes it's the actors, sometimes the writers. This time it was a writer. The first writer was paid off in full, told thanks and goodbye when the scriptlines she had commissioned did not work out. More than 300 people went through casting for the kids' roles. 'I've gone for actors,' Bateman said at the time. 'I haven't cast models and non-professional people.'

But Bateman was smart enough to know that some handsome young people were needed in the cast. Viewers don't want to see the boy or girl from next door. They can see them, acne and all, any time they wish. They are sick and tired of the boy and girl from next door. They want what is commonly known as 'good sorts' and Bateman ensured they got them. 'Heart-throbs are an essential element of a series,' he said. 'The audience wants people to look up to, they want to be involved with the characters. Heart-throbs are just characters people will look up to and care about.'

He didn't add they were people the audience could drool over, but everyone got his general meaning.

The pilot made, the next problem was The Dentist. The Dentist was an extremely important man. His job had nothing to do with extracting molars and filling cavities and worrying about plaque and everything to do with running four television stations, several radio stations and a number of luxury tourist resorts. The name he signed on contracts was Christopher Skase. He was called The Dentist from his fine set of teeth that, because he smiled a lot, and had much to smile about, were more or less permanently exposed like the entire Osmond family going to church.

The Dentist was once a reporter. After working for a financial

'More than 300 people went through casting for the kids' roles'.
The final line-up: (back row, left to right) Sharyn Hodgson (Carly
Morris), Roger Oakley (Tom Fletcher), Vanessa Downing (Pippa
Fletcher), Alex Papps (Frank Morgan), Adam Willits (Steven
Matheson), (front row, left to right) Kate Ritchie (Sally Keating),
Nicolle Dickson (Bobby Simpson) and Helena Bozich
(Lynn Davenport)

newspaper he came to the not unremarkable conclusion that a better future lay in doing the actual deals rather than writing about it. In no time at all, or at least by the age of forty, he was in charge of a chain of broadcasting stations and a chain of marble holiday pavilions where it cost the average weekly wage to lay down the weary head for one night.

Because he was once an everyday hack, he was both admired and envied by other hacks and hackettes, and therefore received a high media profile. This could sometimes be dangerous because the very same hacks, and hackettes, wouldn't mind seeing him fall flat on his gleaming teeth. Or at the very least slip over on a soap.

But The Dentist was determined not to give them that satisfaction. Because he had recently bought the Seven Network, he had many things to prove, not the least that he could run a television network without making foolish mistakes, such as cancelling 'Neighbours'. A successful soap would be just the thing. Along with other executives, The Dentist was shown the pilot of 'Home and Away'. When the lights went on The Dentist's eyes were gleaming as brightly as his teeth. He was so pleased, in fact, he made no effort to hide his excitement and was quick to tell anyone who cared to listen they had just seen the most important development if not since the invention of the wheel at least since the pop-up toaster. And everyone listened because The Dentist paid their wages.

'Go ahead, it's a winner,' said The Dentist. 'Go full steam ahead.'

# The Right Time
# and the Right Place

For a country with a population of only 16 million, Australia produces an extraordinary number of soap operas. It is the McDonald's of soapies, churning them out the way Britain does fine drama and comedies, America situation comedies and police dramas. In 1988, the year 'Home and Away' was launched, the soap department was already well stocked with the three commercial networks screening four locally made serials in prime time – 'Neighbours', 'A Country Practice', 'The Flying Doctors' and 'Richmond Hill'.

Inexpensive to make, they all have healthy ratings, although 'Richmond Hill' was cancelled late in 1988.

Mike Harris, television columnist in the weekly Australian literary and news magazine, the *Bulletin*, recalled Noel Coward's remark on the potency of cheap music when writing on the popularity of soaps. 'Cheap television has power well beyond its worth; you only have to go clicking through the channels in the early evening to demonstrate that. Local domestic drama (i.e. soap) abounds. Indeed, the intensity is such that on four nights a week a viewer can now avoid the news altogether and by some astute channel switching remain neck deep in lather from 6 to 8.30.'

One of the reasons Australia produces so many soaps is a quaint government regulation that forces commercial networks to screen 104 hours of local, prime-time (6pm to 10pm) drama a year, and first run at that. This means they must produce two hours a week. A soap screening for half an hour five nights a week, as do 'Home and Away' and 'Neighbours', exceeds the requirements. The regulation came about because of a need to protect the local industry, there being a large number of thespians who spent more time waiting on restaurant tables or selling socks in department stores than appearing before the camera. Furthermore, because of the predominance of American shows the kids of Australia were sounding like they'd been raised in Brooklyn or Los Angeles.

But even before the regulation came into force in the Seventies, there were a number of local soaps, some highly successful, others remembered only by those with archival minds. The first soap was a meandering serial called 'Bellbird', previously heard as a radio serial, in which the characters never did anything really nasty. It attracted an audience consisting mainly of wearers of rose-coloured spectacles and a number of grandmothers.

Then came the gloriously tacky 'Number 96', set in a block of Sydney flats. 'Number 96' brought everything out of the closet, including homosexuality, rape, nudity and a character called the Phantom Knicker Snipper. One of the leads in 'Number 96' was Sheila Kennelly. She returned to soaps in 'Home and Away'.

A rival network, attempting to outdo 'Number 96', produced a soap called 'The Box', based on the television industry. Judy Nunn played a bisexual journalist called Vicki Stafford. She is also in 'Home and Away'.

From the early days not a year passed without the launch of a new soap. The same was happening in Britain. Determined not to be swamped by soaps from America, where the first, 'One Man's Family', went to air on the NBC network in 1949, the BBC produced 'The Grove Family', first screened in 1954. It was followed in 1960 by 'Coronation Street', which made sitting in front of the television set at 7.30pm on certain days a ritual for millions in Britain. The late John Betjeman, Britain's Poet Laureate, a sophisticated, urbane man, described the ritual as being 'in paradise'.

'Crossroads' began four years after 'Coronation Street'. It has an Australian connection through Reg Watson, who, in his own words, 'produced, directed and edited the serial,' and later created 'Neighbours'.

In recent times 'EastEnders' has challenged and beaten 'Coronation Street' for the attention of viewers.

Most countries now have their own soap industry. In Japan the soaps are called 'home dramas', but unlike British, American and Australian soaps they do not run forever, or, more accurately, they run for as long as viewers remain interested and the ratings hold up. Japanese soaps tend to be full of misery. 'One really has to suffer to be popular in Japan,' observed Ian Buruma, in his book, *The Japanese Mirror*.

In Central and South America soaps are known as telenovelas. Running for 100 or so episodes, they contain the usual soap ingredients. The characters depicted are usually rich, living in a world of wealth and privilege far removed from the misery of the people of the favellas, the slum areas, who are the biggest fans. Brazil's TV Globo, the world's fourth largest network, turns out soaps like a sausage factory, or for that matter a soap factory. Every year they produce six novelas of more than 150 episodes each, assigning roles from a list of 1200 actors and actresses in a computer file, cross-referenced by type: star, protagonist and supporting actor. Storylines are guided by sophisticated viewer polls, the themes changing according to the time of day they are screened. At 6pm TV Globo will show a novela suitable for children, by 10pm they contain murder, corruption, sex and greed.

About 25 million West Germans, and probably a large number from East Germany who can receive capitalist television on their state-manufactured sets, watch 'Schwarzwaldklinik', or 'Black Forest Hospital'. Described as 'schmaltzy', the soap takes Germans back to the time when life seemed easier, but not back as far as the Third Reich.

In the dirt-poor villages of India, people gather around the community television set to watch 'Buniyaad', the story of a family from the First World War through to the late Seventies. More modest in matters sexual than western soaps, it nevertheless looks at the problems of unwed mothers and contraception. So universally popular is 'Buniyaad' that when its producer Amit Khanna visited Parliament during a strike against India's film studios, he found politicians were not interested in the labour problem, only in 'what would happen next in the story'.

So Alan Bateman was following a fine tradition as he gathered around him the ingredients he would blend together to make a soap. And unlike many other television producers, Bateman was not coy about admitting he was in the business of soap operas. He had no hang-ups; it worried him not one bit.

'The thing is, I don't see "soap" as a derogatory term,' he said. '"Brideshead Revisited" was a soap opera. So was "The Forsyte Saga". So were "The Pallisers" and "Upstairs, Downstairs". There are wonderfully cute terms like "contemporary serial" and "Australian drama series" but it's really just a way of categorising. I don't feel ashamed to say "Home and Away" is a soap, because it entertains. A good soap opera does more to inform people, to make them more tolerant, to change attitudes, than all the documentary and current affairs shows have ever done.'

Some might call his statement sacrilege. Or television heresy. Something like that. They would argue a soap could never belong in the same category as a current affairs show.

But on this subject, he is not Robinson Crusoe. His view is supported by Frances Miller, mass medium curriculum consultant in the New South Wales Education Department's Directorate of Studies. She believes soaps fill certain needs of people and can be a way of discussing issues that might be difficult to raise in other circumstances. 'It gives kids the chance to discuss issues like: how do you relate to your parents? How do you form a new relationship? How do you express caring and love? The issues raised in some soap operas are really important to kids. If adults and children sat down together to watch a show that presents matters of concern for kids and adults, that show performs a function.'

The august *New England Journal of Medicine,* discussing the truth that illness is one of the great ingredients of a soap, commented: 'It may well be that daytime serials are the largest source of medical advice in the United States.'

Some scholars have called soaps important cultural documents. They tell much about contemporary life at about the same pace as people live it; in other words they don't suddenly jump a few years as happens in other television dramas; they are a true record. In generations to come scholars will study soaps to learn about the post-Second World War decades as they now pore over scrolls and scrutinise shards of pottery to find the truth about ancient civilisations.

While keeping this in mind, Alan Bateman knew he was in the entertainment business and not that of education. He understood Alfred Hitchcock's statement that 'drama is life with the dull bits left out'.

'If it's not entertaining people won't watch it,' he said. 'Samuel Goldwyn once said: "If you want to send messages, join Western Union." He was right. We don't make message programmes. But at the same time, for "Home and Away" to be successful, it has to be relevant to the audience. If you make a show that is extremely culturally valuable, dealing with real issues, and you've got twee little children dressed up saying twee little middle-class things, then it will have no cultural relevance and, therefore, no relationship to the kids and they just won't watch it. Drama has got to reflect life so it has to be real. Therefore, the things that concern kids today and probably always concerned them – things like getting a job, staying at school, drinking and sex – are all covered as a part of the theme of "Home and Away".'

Especially sex! 'Home and Away' was to find itself in hot water over an episode that involved the suggestion of rape. But such matters were far from Bateman's mind as he worked on the format of the soap.

The producer signed for the series was John Holmes, something of a legend in the Australian soap industry. He produced 'Neighbours' for the Seven Network and briefly for Network Ten. Before 'Home and Away' went to air, Holmes said he had more confidence in the new soap than he had in 'Neighbours'. For instance, it was not restricted to one street as is 'Neighbours'. There was more potential. Holmes had also worked on the Dave Allen and Dick Emery shows and was associate producer on the British-Australian co-productions, 'Father, Dear Father', 'Love Thy Neighbour' and 'Doctor Down Under'.

The writers, headed by series script editor Bevan Lee, a former maths teacher with considerable experience in soaps, gave the characters substance. Research produced a number of stories, some tragic, others positive proof the world is not a place of darkness. Case histories of foster children were studied, portions of which found their way into the soap's subplots.

The idea of using foster children allowed the writers plenty of leeway. The kids all had a past. At any given time the past could come back to haunt them, a theme used in countless books and movies and one

*'Home and Away' follows a fine tradition of 'soaps', but the characters played by Alex Papps (Frank) and Adam Willits (Steve) also have to cope with very real problems ...*

that will continue to be used.

Bateman never forgot the divisions he saw in the unnamed country town. From the beginning he developed that line. In the pilot an aggressive teenage girl called Bobby managed to polarise Summer Bay into those who thought she was an apprentice criminal and those who saw her as an emotionally undernourished little girl.

Also Bateman had his own ideas on how a soap opera should be 'driven' – that is pushed along by the plot or by the characters. He gave an example of a plot-driven soap: 'John falls in love with Karen who turns out to be his uncle's half-sister who left home and came back a millionaire.'

Some soap producers might like this line. Bateman will give it to them for nothing. He was more interested in having the characters move the plots along at a reasonable pace.

And pacey they were. 'I may be accused of wasting time,' he said, jokingly, 'but in the opening episode we meet the Fletchers and the children and go through Tom's sacking and the difficult move to the caravan park – all before the second commercial break. I think that demonstrates a reasonable sense of pace.'

While admitting plot-driven soaps had been successful, they didn't interest Bateman. 'In my view a television series must have some relevance,' he said. 'In character-driven shows, the storyline grows out of the characters. You care about the characters and, therefore, care about their stories.'

He went about creating the settlement of Summer Bay because it was 'a very nice way of looking at the total spectrum of Australia – culturally, economically and racially – and all the other problems that are inherent in Australia too.'

Creating mythical towns, building them in the imagination, establishing businesses and houses, laying out streets, landscaping parks and then seeing them come alive on the screen is a power given to only a few. Soap writers are among them. As one American expert on television said: 'The soap community is a self-perpetuating and self-preserving system – a system little affected by the turbulence experienced by its individual members and fate of any one character.'

Bateman does not give the location of Summer Bay, except that it is on the edge of an urban sprawl. Seeing that 89 per cent of the Australian population live in urban areas and near water it could be anywhere on the edge of the continent, except for the tropical north where sharks, sea snakes and sea wasps reduce swimming to a few winter months. Because 'Home and Away' is made in Sydney, most viewers believe the urban sprawl is that of Australia's largest city.

Dismissing this as unimportant, Bateman said, 'Hopefully it will have no identification within any city in Australia because I am trying to talk about young people in the 1980s, and I think the minute you identify with an area, what you are also saying to kids who live in Brisbane, and Perth and Adelaide, is "Oh, this is not about you." I believe it is critical that you create an environment where you are telling stories about characters and not about places.'

Bateman went to a great deal of trouble to keep the area anonymous. In doing so he created enormous difficulties for the cast and crew who found much of their time was spent in travelling from location to location. The beach scenes are shot at the extremely toffy Palm Beach, Sydney's most northern beach, haven for the rich where visitors are often looked at with a why-are-you-here stare. About forty kilometres inland, at Jackeroo Ranch, Kenthurst, are the caravan park and the Fletcher house. The school is fifteen kilometres closer to the city at Ryde and the interiors of both houses and caravans are shot at the Channel Seven Studios, Epping, a hefty hike of about twenty kilometres from Kenthurst. 'So if you see one of us step out of our caravan and walk on to the beach, we have in fact travelled forty or more kilometres,' said veteran actor Frank Lloyd, who plays Neville McPhee. 'That would have to be the widest beachfront in the world.'

'Home and Away' may have had an unusual plot, but the production crew stuck to the rules as far as the camera work went. A special technique is used for soaps. Close-ups and extreme close-ups are more common than in other television dramas. Explained Bernard Timberg, an American authority on soaps: 'As a narrative ritual that centres on intense, concentrated forms of emotion, soap opera requires an intense intimate camera style ... this close-up camera style has the effect of bringing the viewer closer and closer to the hidden emotional secrets soap-opera explores: stylised expressions of pity, jealousy, rage, self-doubt ... soap opera ritual requires a camera style that circles its characters and brings us closer to them, right up to their eyes and mouths so that we can see their tears and hear their breathing. This is the kind of device that is so

*The stars on location – a location which the shows's creator goes to great lengths to keep anonymous. Top: Alex Papps and Sharyn Hodgson; bottom: Roger Oakley, Adam Willits, Kate Ritchie, Vanessa Downing and Helena Bozich*

taken for granted it escapes our conscious notice while shaping our unconscious response.'

Everything was falling into place. But there was one matter causing grey hairs among Seven Network executives. They had looked at their schedules, argued at length about them and come to the surprising conclusion that 'Home and Away' must be screened at 6pm.

This was surprising for several reasons, not the least that on commercial stations 6pm was reserved for the evening news. In Australia the evening news comes on much earlier than in most countries, a curious situation considering the long summer when the sun is still high in the heavens at 6pm. It is hot outside yet viewers are expected to sit in front of their television sets and watch the carnage, the corruption, the cynicism that has occurred around the world that day. On the other hand Australians go to work earlier than most, many starting at 7am, and by 6pm are home with a cold beer in their hands and their minds ready to receive whatever the news department dishes out.

The executives looked at this. They scrutinised the figures, used words like demographics and target audiences. In the case of 'Home and Away' the target was the eight-to-nineteen-year-old group. They wondered how many of the 4,914,000 Australian TV households owned two sets, for this was the important factor. Parents wanted to watch the news. Kids, hopefully, wanted to watch 'Home and Away'. To avoid family rifts and broken homes, to stop Dad putting an axe through the set because all he could get at 6pm was Summer Bay and not the news, two sets were needed.

Writing on this vexed question, humourist Morris Gleitzman observed: 'Tom and Pippa have got a hell of a job on their hands. Not only have they got to carve out a life for their six foster kids in a run-down caravan park on the South Coast, they've got to do it at the same time of day when for centuries humankind has sat down and watched the news ... I hope they crack it, the Fletchers and the rest of the "Home and Away" team. TV news has been difficult family teatime viewing for a couple of decades now. Across the nation parents are destroying their digestive systems by being on permanent alert with the remote control lest young sensibilities be scarred. Our kids haven't touched dairy food since Margaret Thatcher smiled while they were eating cauliflower cheese.'

Columnist Mike Harris said much the same thing. 'What parents will eventually be drawn to notice is that "Home and Away" is less potentially harmful to their children's psyches than the news programme with their frequent lip-licking coverage of suicide, patricide, homicide and depredation.'

This concern with slotting a soap against the news may seem overblown. But it was extremely important to the Sydney and Melbourne stations of the Seven Network. They hadn't had a good year in 1987, in fact a downright dismal twelve months had just gone by. If 'Home and Away' couldn't be fitted into the 6pm timeslot it was unlikely to get the green light for production.

So the decision was made – 'Home and Away' at 6pm, followed by the news at 6.30pm. Bateman was confident that besides kids the soap would attract a more mature audience who would stay on the same channel for the news, the most important programme for any television station. As he explained: 'From six o'clock on, you start to get people filtering in, people coming home from work, people who are already at home but coming to have their dinner. So your audience profile is changing dramatically through six o'clock, and by the time you reach seven o'clock, which is when the maximum number of sets are in use, you have an audience profile that is largely the Australian demographic.'

As production progressed, Bateman felt confident 'Home and Away' would be a winner. 'I think I've got it right,' he would tell anyone within earshot. 'Of course it will do well.'

But sometimes in the lonely hours of the morning he would wake, his stomach fluttering. He knew the enormity of the task he had taken on. He was aware an entire network was relying on an idea he got when he drove into a country town wanting nothing more than an ice cream.

# 3

# *Casting Problems Hit the Headlines*

The telephone rang in Carol Willesee's home. On the end of the line was her agent, June Cann, with an interesting offer of a lead role in a pilot that, hopefully, would later become a daily serial. Cann felt the role would be ideal for Carol.

'It's for something called "Home and Away",' said Cann.

Carol liked the idea of going before the cameras. It wasn't because she was broke, the cupboards were bare or there was nothing but moths in her purse. Indeed, her financial position was the envy of many. She was surrounded by everything millions of dollars could buy. She lived in a sprawling house in the leafy, well-heeled Sydney suburb of Wahroonga, complete with enormous gardens, swimming pool and tennis courts. Her husband, Michael Willesee, was the nation's most successful current affairs host, not only fronting his own five-night-a-week show but owning the company that made it, thus becoming an inspiration to all television reporters who had ever wanted a wage increase and an expense sheet signed. He also had substantial property investments and a racing stable and stud producing some of the classiest hayburners ever to leap from the starting barriers on Australia's racetracks. She had three children, Amy, then aged eleven, Lucy, ten, and Joey, seven and two large black labradors, Willy and Harry.

There were no dark clouds over Carol Willesee's life. Everything was fine. 'My life is pretty good, actually it's really good,' she said not long before the 'Home and Away' offer was made. 'I have everything a person could want. Sometimes it's a bit frightening to have such a good life because it makes you wonder when you're going to have to pay the dues. I just hope I've already paid mine.'

She owed nothing by way of dues. Born in Scotland, she grew up in a strict Presbyterian household and attended an equally strict school. When she was fifteen her parents separated. As the eldest child, Carol looked after her father, brothers and sisters, leaving school at sixteen to take up modelling. At eighteen she married a young schoolteacher and moved to Singapore but the marriage lasted only four years.

Now came the Australian part of her life. Arriving in Sydney, she decided it was as good a place as any in which to live. She felt relaxed for the first time in many years. She felt free.

She took up modelling again but gave it up when she married Michael in 1976. Being a wife and mother was a fulltime job. But after seven years she got to thinking of earlier ambitions, of her desire to be an actress, to face the cameras, to walk the boards of a stage. On the New Year's Eve of her thirty-fifth year she said to herself, what the heck, it's time to do something about it instead of merely letting it percolate in the mind.

'I had always wanted to be an actress ever since I was young,' she said. 'I gave the idea away a long time ago, but I really wanted to do something before I turned forty. I haven't had a tertiary education and for some reason that left me with a feeling that whatever I had achieved wasn't really worthwhile. I decided no one was going to give me a present and say, "Here you are, this is what you were made for."'

Sitting down she wrote out a list of all the things in which she was interested, crossing them out one by one as she argued with herself over them. Only acting was left. She talked it over with her husband. He knew well the lure of show business, having been in it for most of his working life. Two of his brothers, Terry and Don, were also heavily involved in television. He thought it not a bad idea, and agreed with Carol the best way to go about it was to take acting lessons. Carol enrolled at the Ensemble Acting Studios for a three-year course.

The routine at the Willesee household changed dramatically. Michael learned how to operate the microwave oven because Carol wasn't always there at mealtimes. When she was home she would learn her lines over the stove. 'A bit like those women in TV commercials, stirring the pot with one hand and learning the lines at the same time. I got a buzz out of that.'

After graduating, her first professional role was in the Ensemble Theatre's production of 'Never In My Lifetime'. She received the sort of reviews many actors never get in a lifetime in the business.

After the play's season ended the offers flowed in to her agent. Carol looked at each one. Because she was not in need of money she turned them down on the grounds they were unsuitable, not so much because of the roles but because of her position.

She had always been an extremely public figure. When newspaper editors wanted a series on 'How I Cope With a Famous Husband', they would tell the reporter: 'Ring Carol.' When they wanted an article on 'What I'm Buying My Husband For Christmas', they would say: 'Get hold of Willesee's missus.'

Carol usually obliged. She was that sort of person. So she knew she had to be very selective when accepting a role. 'I knew I would attract a lot of attention because of who I am, so I wanted as good a start as I could possibly get.'

At the same time Michael was laid low by a virus and was forced off camera. Because he was rundown he could not shake it easily, which because he was in show business inspired all sorts of curious rumours. He'd had a breakdown. He'd caught something strange when filming in Asia. He'd fallen in a sewer in Asia and caught something even stranger. None of this was true but it kept the tabloid newspapers happy. A tabloid is not interested in your ordinary, old-fashioned virus, not when there's a possibility of something exotic in the system.

To help with Michael's recovery, the Willesees holidayed on the Barrier Reef and on their return came the approach from the producers of 'Home and Away' for Carol to play the role of Pippa Fletcher. She read the outline of the character: 'Pippa is a calm, self-confident woman with a heart as big as a mountain. The fact that she was unable to have children for medical reasons only serves to make her more determined to open her arms and her home to those who need her. She fell in love with Tom

*Vanessa Downing, who plays Pippa Fletcher – a smiling star now,*
*but she got the part following a blaze of controversy*

the moment she set eyes on him – he was a friend of her brother's, but treated her like a little sister. Years later they met again, to fall in love and marry. When Tom came up with the idea of becoming foster parents, Pippa found herself with a difficult choice to make. If they went ahead with the plan, she'd have to give up her job and become a fulltime mum to other people's children. But Tom's happiness came first with her so she gave up her job and they applied for their first child. She's come to love every one of their foster children and now can't imagine life without them.'

*Singer and classical actress though she is, Vanessa Downing (above, with her screen husband Roger Oakley) thinks 'Home and Away' is 'not a potboiler ... its characters and stories are real and solid, and that's what makes it great'*

*Justine Clarke, who has been verbally abused many times
because of her role as Ruth Stewart*

*Adam Willits, who as Steve Matheson may be one of the youngest heart-throbs in television history*

*Kate Ritchie plays Sally Keating –*
*and doesn't think she's old enough to be a star*

*Alex Papps with his screen foster mother, Vanessa Downing*

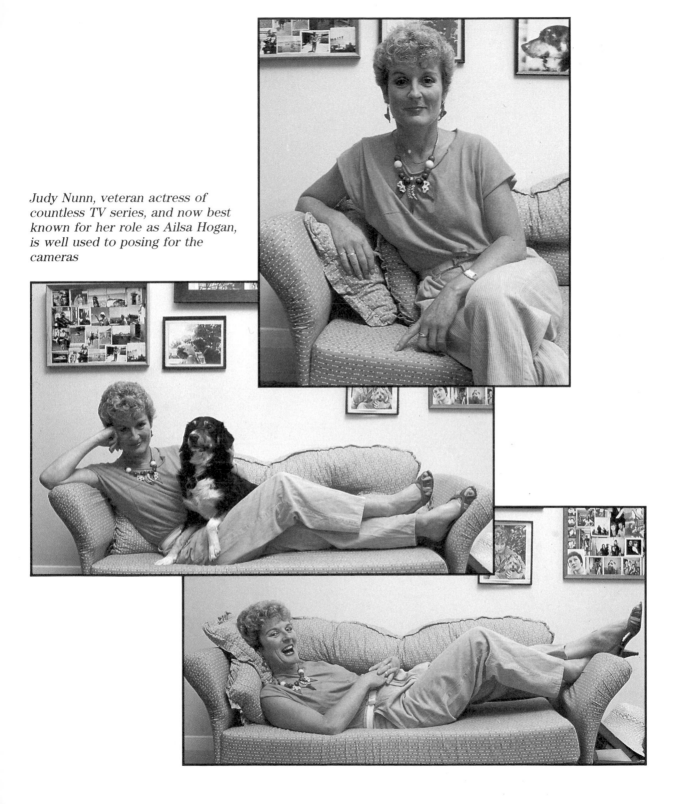

Judy Nunn, veteran actress of countless TV series, and now best known for her role as Ailsa Hogan, is well used to posing for the cameras

*Nicolle Dickson, who is only just getting used to the star treatment that playing Bobby Simpson has meant for her*

*The attention Alex Papps has had as Frank Morgan has changed his life for ever …*

*Will Bobby and Frank
end up together? Nicolle
Dickson and Alex Papps
pose for the cameras*

Carol read and re-read the script. So did Michael. She turned to Michael and said, 'I like it. I can identify with the role.'

Michael agreed. 'It's perfectly suited for you. Why don't you try out for the part?'

'I will,' said Carol. 'The only problem is the hours. I don't want to be away from the children. I'll make sure there's some special clauses in the contract that allow me time off during school holidays and so forth.'

'Looks like it's back to the microwave for me,' said Michael.

'Do you good,' said Carol.

The auditions were held. After eliminating those who perhaps didn't understand Pippa was a mum, not a grandmother or a truckdriver, the choice was between five actresses, including one of great experience, Vanessa Downing.

Carol got the job. 'She has a big future in television,' said producer John Holmes.

She also had the ability to create headlines, a fact not missed by the producers. The newspapers were full of stories about Carol Willesee taking the role, not so much because she was Carol but as Michael's wife. 'Willesee Wife in TV Role' one headline shouted chauvinistically.

Two days later the headlines were to be even larger and noisier.

On Monday she began filming the pilot of 'Home and Away'. She was pleased with the way it had worked out, more so because she had spoken to the producers about the importance of her real-life family. 'I wanted a bit of time to spend with the girls during school holidays,' she said. 'Certainly not all the holidays – just a week. The series would have gone into recess over Christmas, so I was looking at the other school holidays. I was under the impression a contract had been worked out.'

It hadn't. On Wednesday she left the set in tears, never to return. 'You do not make television programmes between 9am and 3.30pm,' snapped Alan Bateman.

Her dismissal produced the sort of headlines reserved for the Second Coming or Australia beating England at cricket. 'Willesee Wife Quits' said the chauvinistic newspaper. 'Carol Loses TV Role' said another.

She drove straight to Michael's office to talk it over with him, her eyes taking in the newspaper billboards already on the streets. She tried not to read the stories over the next few days because Michael warned her they could add to the hurt. But she couldn't help seeing the headlines.

The arguments over her dismissal went on for weeks in newspapers and magazines which relished a television crisis, for this is what it was now made out to be.

'I'm a mother and a wife and my family must come first,' said Carol. 'What happened is that for some reason beyond my comprehension I didn't see the contract until the weekend before I started filming. When I did the auditions and screen test I was told my contract was for one year. I was given verbal assurance that things like my kids' school holidays and my working hours would be amenably looked at. When I finally got my schedule I suddenly realised how long the hours would be. Then I saw the contract and, instead of it saying a year, it said fifty-two production weeks; fifty-two production weeks could be for three years if they wanted to do thirteen weeks then lay off and do another thirteen weeks, and so on. I asked for a couple of clauses to be put into my contract – one of them being that from the starting date the contract was to be for a year. Another was that I could have off a part of school holidays to spend with my kids. Another clause was to be that once or twice a week I'd be able to leave home a little later than 6am and sometimes get home at 6pm, again so I could see the kids. When I saw the contract and the heavy workload expected of me I sat down with the producers and my agent and tried to work out a compromise, but that was impossible. It's such a shame because I was loving the part and the crew and cast had formed a real bond. I'm sorry I caused so much trouble and I hope everything goes well for the show.'

Then Carol made a telling statement. She had been living in an atmosphere where deals were done by shaking hands, an old-fashioned method but one favoured by such media moguls as Kerry Packer. For instance, Paul Hogan did nothing more than shake hands when agreeing to work for Packer's television station. Michael Willesee had done much the same thing. 'It would be wonderful,' Carol said wistfully, 'to shake hands on an agreement but, unfortunately, we live in an age where bits of paper are the things that count. I hope this is not damaging to my career … it would be far worse if it was damaging to my family.' Unfortunately real life often mirrors soap life – Carol and Michael separated early in 1989.

The Seven Network had mixed feelings over Carol's departure. The headlines had provided excellent publicity. The public knew a show called 'Home and Away' was in production and it hadn't cost the network a penny for promotion, not a cent to entertain notoriously thirsty and continually hungry showbusiness journalists. On the other hand a delay in production cost money, making Alan Bateman more than a little unhappy. 'What we cannot accommodate is someone who says I *might* be available for the rest of the year but there *may* be a family crisis and I *may* not be available. It's an intolerable position.'

But the show must go on. And so it came to pass that on the same day Carol Willesee was told her services were no longer required, the telephone rang in the Sydney home of Vanessa Downing. It will be noted the telephone rings frequently in soap stories, not only for the cameras but in real life.

It was her agent. 'Can you take over the lead in "Home and Away?"' the agent asked. 'The actress they'd cast has decided not to go on with it.'

'You mean the role of Pippa?'

'That's the one,' said the agent. 'You start tomorrow.'

'I thought I'd kissed it goodbye,' said Vanessa, remembering she had been in the final five who had auditioned for the role that went to Carol Willesee. And then she had to think for a moment or two because she was working nights in another job – singing with The Madrigirls, a six-women *a capella* group that combined singing with off-beat humour and whacky dress sense. It was doing nice business at the Sydney Opera House.

But a role in a pilot that could go on to become a weekday serial was too good an opportunity to be missed. The opportunity does not often arise. 'I'll be there,' said Vanessa.

At 5.30 the next morning, still in a state of shock, Vanessa was on her way to the Channel Seven studios in the Sydney suburb of Epping.

'When I arrived for filming, everyone was so embarrassed,' she said. 'They thought I would feel bad because I was second choice. But I was glad of the experience because I'd had so little screen work.'

She now had two jobs, an unusual position for anyone in show business. After working twelve hours on 'Home and Away' she would rush to the Opera House to perform with The Madrigirls. 'At one stage I was working twenty hours a day. Fortunately it only lasted three weeks and the pilot episode was completed. We shot the two-hour pilot in three weeks, which is very fast going, but they still took a lot of care.'

Of course, the signing of Vanessa produced more publicity for 'Home and Away'. Naturally she was asked about Carol Willesee's departure. Vanessa obliged. 'I think Carol found it a little more than she had expected to cope with – timewise. I don't think she knew what to expect. She'd done one professional play, as far as I know, so she was very inexperienced. I mean, I was daunted by the schedule and I am experienced, so I don't blame her. She really wanted to do it, I think, and I feel sad for her. I think it's a great shame her first big break had to be such a big job. It would have been much better for her had it been something smaller.'

Said Carol: 'I wish her the best of luck.'

On paper, Vanessa seemed an unlikely choice. Although she had appeared in such Australian soaps as 'Sons and Daughters' and 'The Restless Years', she was considered a 'serious' actress who had got her masters degree in English literature at Sydney University and tutored there while attending acting classes.

She didn't even have a very high opinion of soaps. 'I don't have much time for the endless and unbelievable stream of murders, blackmail and silly love stories you find on some soaps,' she declared, all but committing soap blasphemy. 'I don't really care for the Dynasty-type programmes where events become more and more ridiculous.'

As publicity people winced and wondered if she could be charged with treason, Vanessa turned diplomat. '"Home and Away" is like a slice of real life. It's not a pot-boiler. Its characters and stories are real and solid and that's what makes it great.'

The publicity people relaxed. Here was this actress who had appeared in important productions of 'Who's Afraid of Virginia Woolf?' and 'The Threepenny Opera', who had a masters degree in English literature to boot and was therefore no bimbo, saying this particular soap wasn't all that bad. Back to lunch. There was no need to worry.

But what about her age? She was, after all, much younger than Pippa. 'I think of myself as a character actress,' she replied, 'I'm not anyone's idea of a glamorous leading lady. Over the years I've played everything from a girl of seventeen to a sixty-five-year-old derelict woman. I'm thirty-one, so I suppose I worry a little that people might get an image of me as a mother and an older woman from the show. I'd still like to play Juliet some day, but that doesn't mean I can't play Pippa.'

Even though she works long hours in 'Home and Away' Vanessa still keeps singing at night if possible, not so much for the money but for the sheer pleasure. 'Group singing is enormously therapeutic. I remember I was out of work for ten months once and I joined the Sydney Philharmonic Choir. It literally saved me from depression. So after working at the television studio all day, it's nice to be able to do this at night. It's a wonderful way of ridding oneself of tension. It's very calming, and a lot of fun.'

What Vanessa Downing did in her spare time was of no interest to Alan Bateman and John Holmes as they strove to get the pilot of 'Home and Away' to the screen. After three years' preparation the actual production was completed in the sort of time that would have brought a smile to the lips of old Sam Katzman, the master of Hollywood quickies.

But 'Home and Away' was not just a quickie. The Seven Network was determined it should be a serial, although at this stage they were not publicly admitting it. Television stations do not like admitting much about future plans on the grounds rivals might try to do something similar. Which is often the case.

'We're not looking at it as a pilot,' Bateman said cautiously as it went into production. 'People tend to make their own judgements on that basis. What we are doing is making a quality telefeature which will stand on its own. If it works then we may spin off.'

'Home and Away' did, of course, spin off, as they say in the television industry. But there were some nerve-wracking times to come.

At least the cast was finalised. The original list went like this:

| | | |
|---|---|---|
| TOM FLETCHER | ——————— | Roger Oakley |
| PIPPA FLETCHER | ——————— | Vanessa Downing |
| FRANK MORGAN | ——————— | Alex Papps |
| CARLY MORRIS | ——————— | Sharyn Hodgson |
| STEVEN MATHESON | ——————— | Adam Willits |
| LYNN DAVENPORT | ——————— | Helena Bozich |

| | | |
|---|---|---|
| SALLY KEATING | —————— | Kate Ritchie |
| BOBBY SIMPSON | —————— | Nicolle Dickson |
| ALF STEWART | —————— | Ray Meagher |
| AILSA HOGAN | —————— | Judy Nunn |
| FLOSS McPHEE | —————— | Sheila Kennelly |
| NEVILLE McPHEE | —————— | Frank Lloyd |
| RUTH STEWART | —————— | Justine Clarke |
| DONALD FISHER | —————— | Norman Coburn |
| LANCE SMART | —————— | Peter Vroom |
| MARTIN DIBBLE | —————— | Craig Thomson |
| CELIA STEWART | —————— | Fiona Spence |

# Launch of a Super-Soap

Journalists assigned to the television rounds would rather not travel second class. This is clearly understood by the television industry which made the discovery many years ago that the said journalists prefer French champagne to domestic, a lobster to a ham sandwich. So the spread laid out for journalists for the launching of 'Home and Away' at a plush restaurant could be fairly described as sumptuous.

Held on a balmy night in mid-January, 1988, the location was the Flamingo, a very desirable venue on the edge of Palm Beach, the far northern suburb of Sydney where the extremely rich, like Kerry Packer, live and play and not far from the home of actor Bryan Brown and his British actress wife, Rachael Ward. It was the perfect spot for the party; after all, 'Home and Away' uses Palm Beach's long sweep of golden sand and calls it Summer Bay.

The launching featured a number of extracts from the soap. Fiona Spence, who plays Aunt Celia, watching the preview with other members of the cast, became a trifle edgy. None of her scenes were included in the footage. Furthermore, she was not introduced to the gathering.

The gathering, of course, knew her quite well. 'How's Vinegar Tits?' someone asked her.

To call her by such a vulgar name was not an insult. She had earned the title by playing a tough wardress who came across like an SS officer in the long-running soap, 'Prisoner'.

Fiona wondered if she should start worrying about her exclusion from the preview clips and the fact she was not introduced. Was it time for a touch of paranoia which exists in show business the way sore backs do in the removalist business? Or was it just an oversight?

In fact, it was an oversight. 'Oh, well,' said a relieved Fiona, 'that's show business.' And she got back to the business of celebrating with everyone else.

Included among everyone else was a large number of young people, a fact not lost on the journalists. There were kids who looked as if they should have been home occupying themselves with school studies rather than swanning about in flash restaurants.

'More lambs to the slaughter,' said one cynic, extending his arm for another glass of champagne.

'Give 'em a year,' said his equally cynical colleague. 'You'll never hear of 'em after that.'

In some ways the cynicism was not out of place. With a few remarkable exceptions – the names of Kylie Minogue and Jason Donovan, of 'Neighbours', spring immediately to mind – the young soapie stars flash briefly across the screen, then vanish into some vast black hole. They join the legion of the disappeared. The truth of this was seen late in 1988 when 'Richmond Hill' was suddenly axed, teaching four young stars that show business and security do not walk hand in hand. They learned early in their careers that they were little more than commodities to be used by a certain date.

But the lure of show business is strong. None of the 'Richmond Hill' kids would admit to being disenchanted. 'I'm sick and tired of the conservatives saying you should do school,' said fifteen-year-old Marc Gray. 'If I want to do my Higher School Certificate, I'll go back and do it because acting is a once-in-a-lifetime experience.'

One problem facing kids who have appeared in a soap, then find themselves out of work, is the stigma attached to soaps. Some producers do not consider it respectable work. Said eighteen-year-old Ashley Paske, from 'Richmond Hill', 'Within the acting industry people always say, "If

*Fiona Spence (second from left) 'Vinegar Tits' in the tv series
'Prisoner' but now better known as 'Home and Away's' Celia
Stewart, stars in Summer Bay's Nativity performance. Her co-star
is Lance Smart, played by Peter Vroom (second from right)*

you're doing soap you should stay in it for a certain time and then get
out." But obviously you don't because you are enjoying it and you're
learning. So it's not a Brecht/Shakespeare script but it's television drama.
We work hard, we produce work very quickly and we do our best.'

The sudden fame is also a problem. Some cope, some don't. One year
they can be at school, the next a face known around the world. Alan

Bateman put it this way when talking about the ability of young people to cope with sudden fame: 'It's one of those things you don't actually take in until it happens. One day you're a novice actor and in a few months you become an Australian star ... And then you're an international star. It is difficult to imagine.'

However, such thoughts were not worrying the kids of 'Home and Away' at the launching party. They weren't looking too much into the future. A few would become household names but some would not make it through the year, at least not on television and would be asking the whereabouts of the nearest dole office. The only thing concerning them right then was the nice contracts they had in their pockets which paid them around $A1,000 a week, not a fortune but much more than the sums earned by their rivals on 'Neighbours' when they began their soapie climb to fame. After a year with 'Neighbours' Kylie Minogue was getting little more than $A300 a week, the adults lucky to take home $A1,000. It was a pittance and caused some embarrassment to the Grundy Organisation, producers of 'Neighbours', when the press revealed the figures.

After the launching party, when the last of the good food and booze had been cleared away, the crew and cast waited tensely for the critics' opinions of the show. When they appeared within the next week or so everyone let out a sigh of relief. With one or two exceptions, the reviews were kind, even enthusiastic.

Robin Oliver, of the *Sydney Morning Herald,* said, 'The exceptionally well-constructed serial looks destined for a long and important run. ... All up: easily the best five-night serial in years.'

Elizabeth Swallow, of the *Australian*, called it 'competently made' with 'first-class production skills, good acting, credible characters and situations'.

Louise Stephenson, of the *Sydney Daily Telegraph*, thought there was 'something about the Fletchers and Summer Bay that pulls at the old heartstrings'.

Mike Harris of the *Bulletin*, said, 'So patently well-intentioned is the purpose behind the basic story that it would be churlish to criticise it, save to remind that it is designed with an eye towards the ratings.'

Frank Gauntlett, of the *Sydney Daily Mirror*, argued there was little purpose served 'by mercilessly bagging soaps. They are an all too easy target judged by standards to which they do not aspire, they keep a lot of people in work and even more people harmlessly amused.'

One critic, namely this writer, was surprised a soap could survive in a setting that included a caravan park. 'I have nothing against caravan parks but they are hardly places of high drama,' I wrote in my *Sunday Telegraph* television column. 'On the few occasions I have stayed at caravan parks, the only dramas were a blocked toilet and a 3am argument between the couple in the Viscount next door. But I don't suppose this matters much to the producers of soaps. A soap producer could make a blocked dunny [lavatory] last a week and turn an early morning domestic into a United Nations debate on world security.'

Perhaps my opinion was coloured by the fact that I dislike caravans. There are about 50,000 registered caravans in New South Wales and every one seems to be on the road just ahead of me, causing an alarming surge in blood pressure as they sway along at a speed well below the limit.

The Seven Network could do little more now than hope people would tune in at 6pm to hear the mawkish title song introducing 'Home and Away' which sounded as if it had been written in some lonely attic by a tear-stained composer who did little else than write maudlin Saturday night tunes for TV. If they stayed with the show for the next half hour it would be even better.

They didn't. Not at first. Alan Bateman, along with Seven Network executives, looked at the early ratings figures and shuddered. It was getting a rating of twelve. Now a rating of twelve is a figure good for little else than sobbing over while cutting the wrists. A discussion on Hittite pottery might be expected to get a rating of twelve, not a relatively expensive soap.

Bateman and others began clutching at straws. They carefully perused the fan mail and saw therein hopeful signs. They read reports from the publicity department which said the cast was well-received at public appearances at shopping centres. They might not have gone as far as studying the leaves in tea cups or the spread entrails of a fowl as a guide to the future, but they did take some heart from the soap's performance in Perth, a far outpost of the Seven Network.

Boasted Bateman: 'The battle has been waged in Perth where "Home and Away" was up against "Neighbours", the only place the two shows have gone head to head. On one episode (featuring a wedding) we rated thirty-seven and "Neighbours" scored a three.'

Network Ten hurriedly moved 'Neighbours' out of the competition.

But slowly the ratings built up, after about six months, reaching towards a figure of twenty in the important market of Sydney, then hitting twenty-five. 'Home and Away' was home and safe.

Several months after it first went to air the soap was sold to Britain's ITV which had noted the success of 'Neighbours' on the BBC and wanted something similar, or preferably better in attracting an audience. 'It is a great acknowledgement of the quality of "Home and Away",' said Bateman, who could never be judged guilty of hiding his light under a bushel. 'I have always been very confident the subject matter we deal with is universal. The issues that affect the young and families are the same in Britain as in America and Germany and Australia: the issues of single-parent families, foster children, unemployment, drugs. The bottom line is the characters are universal characters, interesting, loveable, hateable characters.'

While pleased with the sale of 'Home and Away' to Britain, Bateman expressed no great surprise. In fact he would have been surprised if it had not been sold because he believed that no one made better soaps than Australia. 'We make the best serials in the world,' he said. 'We must do, they sell all over the world.'

With the ratings worry safely behind them, those involved with 'Home and Away' could get on with the deadly serious business of conjuring up the twists and turns necessary to keep a soap frothing nicely along. Robin Oliver in the *Sydney Morning Herald* gave an insight into the way writers work: 'Down by the banks of the Paramatta River at Rydalmere [a Sydney suburb] a group of five writers has turned its back on what is a rather restful view, tucked into fish and chips from its favourite shop in Victoria Road, and begun contemplating episode 68 of the television serial, "Home and Away". It's a serious business, and means developing a mind's-eye view of the coastal resort of Summer Bay and a caravan park that could be almost anywhere in four States ...

'There's a tricky moment ahead – a minor cliff-hanger involving young love and the attempted seduction of Alex Papps – who plays the good-looking young hero, Frank – by another character who keeps pleading her virginity, but who we already know is pregnant...

'Every now and then the five take a breather by conjuring up vulgar variations of the seduction scene – suggestions which would be quite unsuitable for "six o'clock parlance" – the carefully modified language required by an early evening audience divided between teenagers and the over-fortys...'

After eight months 'Home and Away' was no longer a matter of concern for Seven Network executives. They became more relaxed each week as they noted the ratings. They were congratulating themselves on the success of their bold experiment in screening the soap at 6pm, telling each other what splendidly astute fellows they all were, when they were hit by a bombshell.

Alan Bateman, the man who thought up the idea and carried it through to success, the man some called the Drama King, resigned from the Seven Network and switched to the Nine Network. To the television industry it was as stunning as Margaret Thatcher suddenly stepping into Neil Kinnock's shoes.

Or as Bateman himself put it: 'It was fearful, dreadful. Plato said all change causes pain. He was right.'

Seven was furious. Christopher Skase (The Dentist) and other senior executives flew immediately from Brisbane to Sydney to see what could be done and to kick a few behinds for allowing it to happen, but it was too late. Nine had Bateman signed and sealed.

The Nine Network badly needed someone of Bateman's talent. It had not produced a successful daily serial for more years than it cared to remember, prompting this tepid joke: In case of nuclear warfare run to Nine's drama department 'cos they haven't had a hit in years.

Alan Bond, the Perth entrepreneur behind Swan and XXXX beers, the man who took the America's Cup, symbol of world yachting supremacy from the United States and lost it back four years later, had bought the Nine Network for an extremely high price and he wanted results. He didn't appreciate jokes about Nine's drama department. Furthermore he had a dislike of coming second.

'Get the best man for the job,' he ordered from his Perth base.

The best man was Bateman. He was got.

After he had settled into Nine and the dust there, if not at Seven, had cleared, Bateman said, 'I'll always have a special affection for "Home and Away" – it would be a lie if I said I wouldn't – and I hope it will continue to be a winner. But I'll tell you this, we'll be doing another winner. I have one or two up my sleeve.'

He certainly had. A few months later he was responsible for another bombshell exploding in what was once the secure and comfortable atmosphere of 'Home and Away'.

# 5

# Alex Papps – Heart-Throb

Alex Papps was jumpy. The crowd was pushing in on him and other cast members of 'Home and Away', bustling, shoving, mauling, at times using elbows and fists to get closer, to touch the stars. It was a crowd on the edge of hysteria. The crowd's reaction was nothing new. Crowds had been mauling soapie stars ever since they were placed on the same pedestals as pop stars. But in recent times those receiving the attention have reported a new threat – to the more personal parts of the anatomy.

'You know,' said one soapie star who preferred to remain anonymous, 'I was signing autographs in a crowd when I felt a hand on my crotch. Just like that. Looking right at me with a smile on her face was a kid, she wouldn't have been more than fourteen. Butter wouldn't have melted in her mouth. Yet she was grabbing me like I was her lover or something. You wouldn't believe it.'

Something similar happened to Greg Benson, the handsome young man who plays Matt the Surfie in 'Home and Away' when he was appearing at a shopping centre in the western Sydney suburb of Blacktown. 'We were walking Greg through the crowd when all of a sudden he doubled over. We got quite a shock because we weren't sure what happened at first,' said Channel Seven publicist Gary Farrar. 'But apparently he'd been groped rather savagely in a very private place by a young girl whose hand somehow came up from below – so she must have been on her knees, or very short. It shook Greg up quite a bit, understandably. Not even the bodyguards were prepared for an attack from below.'

Alex Papps wasn't keen on these promotional outings, usually held at vast suburban shopping centres. The idea had originated with the publicity people behind 'Neighbours' who had worked out that shopping centres attract around 1.5 million people a week in Sydney alone. Shopping centres, soapie stars and hysterical crowds soon became a ritual on Saturday morning and during late-night shopping. But this didn't make it any easier for the young stars and while Alex was being buffeted, at the same time signing autographs as fast as his tired arm would allow, John Lennon's name crossed his mind. Poor, dead Lennon. Shot by a stranger, killed by an unknown face in the crowd.

'Look, I'm not egotistical enough to believe someone would want to assassinate me,' said Alex. 'But there are people with strange mental disorders out there who are so unpredictable, so menacing, you just have to be careful … whoever you are.'

Of course Alex is not alone when it comes to worrying about the obsessiveness of fans. On several occasions the cast of 'Neighbours' has had to be rescued by police from enthusiastic fans. They are used to it but it doesn't make them feel any better about it. For someone experiencing a hysterical mob for the first time it can be a traumatic experience. Nicolle Dickson, who plays Bobby Simpson in 'Home and Away', broke down and cried the first time she was mobbed. It happened at a Brisbane shopping centre and the disturbance left two fans injured. 'It's very obsessive,' she said. 'It's scary to think people can be overwhelmed by you. The trip to Brisbane was the first time I'd experienced anything like that. We got out of these limos, people screamed and it really put me on edge. I felt I was about to break down. I couldn't believe it. It suddenly hit me because when you go to work each day at the studio you don't think of the effect you're going to have.'

The attention afforded Alex Papps is understandable. He is to 'Home and Away' what Jason Donovan is to 'Neighbours'. For better or worse, he is the sex symbol of 'Home and Away', the heart-throb if you like, but

*Like it or not (and when mobbed by fans in supermarkets he doesn't like it) – Alex Papps/Frank Morgan is a sex symbol*

it is not a title he wears with comfort. 'I hate it when I'm referred to as a heart-throb. It is the antithesis to what I believe I'm all about. I try not to let it influence my way of thinking. People always need to label you, even if it is as a heart-throb, an idiot or a dag. Other people need the labels, I don't. ... It's a weird feeling. I don't really know how to deal with it. I know me and I know I'm not a particularly macho male. It's difficult sometimes to know what people expect you to look like and be like.'

But he can't escape the label. Even his character, Frank Morgan, is described as a heart-throb. Says the show's summary of the character: 'Eighteen-year-old Frank, with his streetwise ways, disarming smile and rock and roll ambitions, is a real heart-throb. His father was a professional criminal, his mother an alcoholic. He became a street kid ... petty crimes brought him to the attention of the authorities. When they discovered his father was in prison and his mother was incapable of looking after him, Frank was fostered out to Tom and Pippa. He was eight years old. Although Frank was street smart, he wasn't academically bright ... and only just managed to scrape through his exams up to Year 10. The only thing he was good at was playing guitar.

'Through the [welfare] department, Tom and Pippa knew that Frank's father had never given up trying to find him. While he was still under the jurisdiction of the department, they were able to deny him access, but once he came of age, Tom and Pippa told Frank the decision was his. He doesn't want to see either of his parents again. Right now his main concern is finding a job and forming a band.'

Alex was eighteen when he joined the cast of 'Home and Away'. But even at that age he was a show business veteran. 'My parents didn't allow me to get an agent until Year 7,' he joked.

He was born into an artistic environment, his parents both involved in local theatre in the Dandenongs, on the outskirts of Melbourne. His parents typify the multi-cultural society of Australia where immigration since the Second World War has given the country people from around the world a melting pot of races, languages and religions. Alex is proud of his background. 'My father's name is Apollo, he's Greek but he was born in Cairo. My mother's English on her mother's side but Jewish on her father's side. My parents are teachers. But they have both been involved in theatre since before I was born.'

He had minor roles in the long-running soapie, 'Prisoner', and 'Neighbours' in the days before it became an international success. In 'Neighbours' he is remembered as the kid who burned down Charlene's caravan. But even then he wasn't really bitten by the acting bug. This happened when he was cast in 'The Henderson Kids', one of those family situation shows that abound on television, literally plucked from the school yard for the role. Four months of filming took its toll on study, but his college lecturer was assigned as tutor for the young cast, helping him through his school years.

Then he became Frank Morgan. Within weeks his life had changed in a way he had never thought possible. Of all the cast of 'Home and Away', he was the one singled out for attention, the slightly built teenager with the Tom Cruise smile. 'It's true, I've seen them run right over other people to get to him for autographs and to take pictures of him,' a Seven spokesperson said.

He was mobbed at shopping centres. At a country race meeting he was followed everywhere by a curious crowd of small boys, adoring girls of all ages and even a few camera-toting mothers. At first puzzled by the attention, he tried to work out the reasons and rationalise that it was all a part of the fantasy of television.

'It's still a very strange feeling,' he said. 'It is nice to know that people react to what you do, but I don't really know how to cope with it. I remember when it started to happen. I found it was strange to think people knew about you and saw your face in magazines. The way I've worked it out is that the person who is being seen in the magazines or on television is a totally separate part of me. That is the way I'm trying to stay detached from it. I think I have to try and maintain that separation in what is the television person and what is me.'

Then he became troubled by the attention. He questioned the values surrounding popularity, the importance of a soapie character compared with the real person. Sometimes he claimed to be another person when he was approached in the street for an autograph.

'No, I'm afraid you've got the wrong person,' he would say, as a fan came towards him, autograph book or scrap of paper in hand.

The fan would stop, hesitant. The fan knew that if it wasn't Frank Morgan, or perhaps Alex Papps, then there was a dead-ringer strolling about town. Sometimes it worked but he didn't like doing it, a feeling of guilt coming over him because he well knew that without fans he would be just another actor striving to make a buck.

'I suppose people can take it as being snobbish but it's not,' he said. 'It's just that sometimes you are caught off-guard and you try to get out of the situation as easily as possible. It's silly, I suppose.'

Yet at other times he would encourage fans to stop and talk with him. It was the pushy ones that upset him. 'A lot of people you see in the street seem to think you're up yourself, or a snob, or you will talk down to them. However, the gratifying thing is when you talk to people, whether they be children, teenagers or whatever, it's lovely to find they are very much at ease. They soon realise you're not so very special. You're not the snob they thought you were.'

His problem, if indeed it could be called such, was that he did not crave the visibility of young television stars like Jason Donovan and Kylie Minogue. He was interested in acting, not glamour and stardom. 'The publicity side of what I do worries me,' he said. 'It can become so big that it appears more important than the show itself. Glamour and all of that are things that happen in Hollywood. They are illusions a lot of the time and have nothing to do with the work itself. Obviously I would like to have the status of somebody like Robert De Niro or Meryl Streep. Who in this business wouldn't want to be as good as De Niro?'

He began to resent the intrusions fans made into his life. It came to a head in Brisbane at Expo '88 when he was confronted by a bossy young woman with a camera.

'Come on, do this,' she shouted at Alex.

He obliged. 'Now do that,' she demanded. 'And this. And that.'

Alex turned on her, his voice angry. 'Who the hell do you think you are,' he shouted back. She seemed surprised at his reaction. Didn't the public own him? Wasn't she a member of the public? She walked away muttering about the rudeness of certain soapie stars who had grown too big for their boots.

Sometimes he worried that fans would find out where he lived and he would find them crawling through his windows. 'I'm prepared to give of myself for the show when necessary, but my house – and my private life – is my own. I don't think that's unreasonable. ... The crowds have made me think about people. It interests me that so many people can get so engrossed in "Home and Away" and in any television show. I wonder what it is in their lives that attracts them so intensely to a television series.'

What made his life more hectic was that he was also co-host of a television show called 'The Factory', three hours of live television screened each Saturday morning, featuring music and interviews for audiences up to the teenage years. It was made in Melbourne and his life became a blur of flying south from Sydney once a week, going to promotions, travelling here and there until he had little idea of even where he was. Aircraft and taxis became places in which to sleep, or at the very least to learn lines. 'I got into acting because I like acting, but there are days when you question your reasons for being in it,' he confessed.

Not only was he tired, but he was painfully homesick. His was a close-knit family but it lived 1000kms from where he was working. They understood this on 'Home and Away' and on his nineteenth birthday gave him a surprise party. In his words: 'I thought there might be something on when I was told there was something waiting for me in the wardrobe department. I walked in and the wardrobe guy pushed me towards a door. I opened it and there was my sister Selena, standing with a big bow tied around her ... I must say I have missed my family.'

Then one year after 'Home and Away' was first screened, a mere twelve months after it first struggled to find favour with viewers, came the bombshell that was obviously ignited by Alan Batemen, who had left Seven and switched to Nine. Alex Papps announced he was leaving the soapie for the more substantial suds of 'The Flying Doctors' a weekly show set in the Australian outback. For a couple of years it had been Nine's main contribution to local drama but although it had scored reasonable ratings, had never reached the figures that cause programme managers to uncork the champagne and do cartwheels along the executive corridor. By bringing Alex across Bateman hoped to change that.

'Alex has been under enormous pressure and he's come out of it a much more mature figure,' said Bateman. 'He's rounded off as an actor and as a consequence he's rounded off as a person. It's this maturity which is reflected in his acting.'

*Fans gasped and the ratings soared on heart-throb Frank Morgan
and Ruth Stewart's wedding day. But it turned out to be the
most famous Wedding That Never Was ...*

Said Alex: 'Doing one hour a week means the pressure isn't as high.'
He was, of course, asked about the dangers of leaving a popular
show, especially one in which his character had been favourably received.

The history of show business is strewn with actors who moved out of hit shows with ambitious intent only to disappear into limbo.

He pondered the question. Then he said, 'You can't let something like a show's popularity be a factor when you're deciding whether or not you should move on to other projects. You can't afford to be blasé.'

On the surface Alex Papps is a calm young man, beneath he is angry. Not with himself, not with his career, but with the world. He sees what governments are doing and wants to lash out. 'That bloody American space programme. I read that the money poured into that could end the famine immediately. I just don't know, there's so many people sitting on mega millions who just don't do enough. Regardless of where my acting career goes over the next few years, the conservation movement is something I'd like to get involved with. One of the reasons I admire Sting and Bob Geldof is their ability to look outside their careers and their own worlds, to take an interest in what's going on in the world.'

Being conservative organisations, owned by the same mega rich he scorns, television networks might take exception to his views. 'Stuff them if they do,' he said. 'It's got nothing to do with them. As long as I don't act in a way that gives them a bad name, I can't see why not. As long as I don't get drunk and chain myself to a tree or something.'

# Justine Clarke – On Playing Ruth

She was only sixteen. She was standing in a crowd in a Sydney shopping centre when a girl pushed her way through. She looked at the sixteen-year-old for a few moments, her face twisted by a mixture of anger and hate and perhaps something else. Something more dangerous.

Then she spoke. Or rather she shouted: 'Slut!'

The word cut through the sixteen-year-old who stepped back in astonishment. She couldn't believe what she had heard. But there was no mistake the second time.

'Slut!' the girl screamed again.

The sixteen-year-old quickly got into her car waiting nearby. 'I started laughing because I thought it was a joke at first,' said Justine Clarke. 'But this girl was real serious. She had this real nasty look on her face. It was awful. We just drove away.'

Justine, who of course was the sixteen-year-old, has been verbally abused many times because of her role in 'Home and Away'. She is television's youngest 'bitch'. She may not be a bitch in the sophisticated style of Joan Collins' character or in the fashion of the interfering old harpy, Mrs Mangel, in 'Neighbours'. But she is a bitch all the same.

The darkest moment for Justine's character, the bitchiest, came when

*Justine Clarke in real life is nothing like her screen character*
*Ruth – known as television's 'youngest bitch'*

she convinced the nice young Frank Morgan that he was the father of her child and demanded he accompany her up the aisle. The audience knew Frank wasn't responsible so they made Justine the target of their hate, thus once more confusing fantasy with reality.

Perhaps there is some excuse for the confusion because in these days of intense promotion, much of it in glossy fan magazines, the characters are written about as though they are real people. The cover lines scream: 'Shock Pregnancy in "Home and Away" or 'Neighbours Stars Divorce'. That sort of thing. The unsuspecting could be forgiven for thinking one of the stars had unexpectedly been put in the family way or an old married couple had decided to follow separate paths. Closer scrutiny reveals the divorces, the pregnancies, happened to characters. Even the actors give lengthy interviews about their characters, speaking of them in the first person as though they exist.

Fact and fantasy become one. Confusion sets in and sixteen-year-old kids are called sluts in public.

The soapie stars quickly learn this is something with which they have to cope. Being accepted as their character, not themselves, is something they learn early in their careers, along with the truths that studying lines is not exactly a ball of fun and soap producers have never heard of the forty-hour week.

'I used to always get booed on stage at functions,' said Justine. 'It was funny at first, people looking at you in the street, but after a while you get used to it. And I thought to myself at least I was getting to my audience.'

Mark Stevens, seventeen, of 'Neighbours', was bashed by a group of thugs who didn't like what they saw on the screen. It was worse when he was in the musical television show, 'Young Talent Time'. 'Because I was singing and dancing some guys thought I was a homosexual and started ribbing me. It happens all the time.'

Said Josephine Mitchell, of 'A Country Practice', 'People can't distinguish between reality and TV.'

Christopher Truswell, who plays Nudge in the Australian family situation comedy, 'Hey Dad', gets upset over the confusion. 'People tend to think you're as naive as your character,' he said. 'People will come up to you and say, "How ya goin' Nudge?" and all that sort of thing. They just want to keep calling you Nudge. I just think, "At least I don't have to hang around these sort of people," but, really, it's all part of the job.'

Even experienced actors can become confused. The American actor, the late Richard Deacon, an unabashed fan of soaps, told the story of the time he was walking past the NBC building in New York when another actor emerged and nodded at Deacon in recognition. Deacon stopped because he knew the man well, or thought he did. They chatted for some time, catching up on gossip and parted promising to arrange lunch together in the near future. As he walked away, it dawned on Deacon he'd never met the other actor before. He was a regular on the American daytime soap, 'Days of our Lives'.

Because she plays a bitch, Justine Clarke gets into more conflict with the public than most on 'Home and Away'. Her armour is her sense of humour. 'It has been a handy weapon as far as playing the bitch is concerned. You have to be ready to defend yourself as nicely as possible. But, really, you cannot afford to take all this too seriously.'

At first Justine tried to live as normally as possible, even to the extent of having her telephone number in the directory. Not surprisingly the phone never stopped ringing. 'I used to get a lot of phone calls because we didn't have a silent number,' she said. 'But we do now. The callers would ask how Frank was, or what was going to happen next in the show, things like that. I would answer their questions as best I could. The thing is, we have to be polite, no matter how rude they might be to us. We do have a certain responsibility to the public, I guess.'

Now she takes precautions to protect herself. She regularly uses a bodyguard to keep away the more unstable members of the public. 'Particularly when we do shopping centres,' she said. 'It's really strange, the knowledge you're in such a position where you need protection.'

And at the tender age of sixteen summers.

Why is this pretty blonde teenager the subject of so much abuse? The answer lies in her character of Ruth (Roo) Stewart, described this way: 'To the adults of Summer Bay, Roo is the ideal teenager. To her peer group, she's a popular little rager. Doted on by her father, Alf, who is over-protective, she's had to work very hard to make sure he doesn't find out that she's not the Miss Goody Twoshoes he fondly imagines her to be. Since puberty, Roo has been boy crazy. ... When she met Frank, the fact that he was a city boy added to the definite attraction between them. Roo has very definite ideas about what is and isn't good for her dad – as far as she's concerned, no woman could ever fill her mother's shoes, especially not Ailsa Hogan. She has no qualms about interfering until the relationship falls apart.'

Justine has been working in television for as long as she cares to remember, inspired by her parents who were both in show business. Her mother, Beverley, was an actress and dancer, her father, Len, a singer. She was appearing in commercials at the age of seven, was a semi-regular in 'A Country Practice' and one of the feral kids in 'Mad Max III', with Mel Gibson. After finishing playing the lead role in the telemovie, 'Touch The Sun', produced by the Australian Children's Television Foundation, she holidayed with her family in Thailand and Bali where she lay back in the sun and contemplated her future. Right then it seemed mostly to involve preparing herself for her Higher Schools Certificate years – until she auditioned for the part of Roo in 'Home and Away'. The producers had spent a great deal of time and energy searching for the right actress. Teenage bitches do not grow on trees or even under them. But they stopped their search when they auditioned Justine. She was right for the part and on the day her schoolfriends started their summer holidays she began work on the soap.

One of the scenes the writers had planned for her was a wedding. Now weddings are as important to soaps as car chases are to cop shows. Probably more so. You can have a car chase in every episode of a cop show but not a wedding in every soap episode unless it is set in a marriage bureau. Producers and writers treat weddings with a great deal of respect because they can provide tremendous boosts to ratings, not only for the actual ceremony but during the days leading to the nuptials. Will they or won't they make the altar? Will an old lover turn up? Maybe the bride's dress won't arrive on time. Or something will go wrong with the honeymoon. Such matters are the bread and butter of soaps and it is therefore not surprising that producers and writers tend to cluck over weddings like a brood of elderly aunts.

Oscar Whitbread, executive producer of 'The Flying Doctors', which has seen a wedding or two in its time, believes people become involved in a soap wedding the way they do with a royal wedding – it combines romance and fantasy with wholesome morality and furthermore can be spun out over a couple or more weeks. 'I think,' he said, 'it is refreshing and rewarding for an audience to see an institution so important back in favour. They all say, "aw, isn't it nice" and "about time, too". Without weddings and romance, the whole industry would collapse in a heap. When you look at the weekend papers and see the number of people engaged or married, you realise just how important the institution is. I don't think you can put your own value judgements on it.'

No one takes weddings more seriously than Alan Bateman. He can talk at length on the subject of weddings and often does. 'Weddings are vital because there are great heroic moments in the sweep of human experience, always marked by ceremonial events. Births, deaths and marriages are epic benchmarks in people's lives. A wedding in a series is very important because it creates a huge high point.'

But Bateman argues that merely to toss in a wedding to gain an audience is not only unfair but dangerous. 'Anyone who says, "The ratings are in trouble, let's marry somebody" is in deep, deep trouble. The audience will not believe it. But if the characters are well fleshed out, the audience will hope they fall in love with somebody and hopefully it will be consummated in marriage.'

He added, 'It would be great to believe weddings are always based on this consummation of love. But as the wedding of Frank and Roo shows, this is not always the case.'

Indeed not. It was a shotgun wedding and the wrong man was named as the father. Frank was innocent in the matter of putting Roo in the family way. However she convinces Frank he is the father and being a decent sort of chap, if a little naive, he offers to marry her. Roo accepts with some speed.

In full ceremonial gear they arrive at the church, constructed in the studio with no outsiders allowed. They reach the altar. Not a sound can be heard. And then with a quivering lip and tears streaming down her cheeks, Roo saves the day by proving she is not such a bitch as everyone thought.

'I can't,' she blurts out, instead of saying, 'I do.'

With wedding dress flying, she bolts down the aisle, Frank in hot pursuit and not a little confused by the turn of events. Outside the church she falls flat on her face on the front lawn and as Frank dusts her off she tells him the truth. One critic reported it was a two-handkerchief night. Or half a box of tissues.

The wedding not only produced the required ratings but lead to some

*Ruth (played by Justine Clarke) became a more popular character when she owned up to Frank (Alex Papps) and called the wedding off*

discussion. The fan magazines and tabloid newspapers, which had had a field day with such provocative headlines as 'Shotgun Wedding', leapt on Alex Papps and Justine Clarke for comment.

Alex pointed out that although he had nothing against weddings, he wasn't keen on marriage himself, at least not at his age. 'I would hate to be married at nineteen,' he said, adding that marriage wasn't always the solution when someone so young fell pregnant. 'I don't think marriage would solve anything. Socially it looks better because it makes it all look legitimate, but marriage doesn't sort the problem out.'

Justine was of the same opinion. 'It just adds to the complication, especially when you're not sure whether you love the person.'

Marriage itself was understandably far from her mind. 'I couldn't even think of getting married at the moment,' she told an inquisitive reporter. On being pregnant, not her but her character, she said, 'It is a very frightening thing to have to go through … really sad that people have to go through the experience and the way people change their attitudes towards them. I think it's good the show is on at the time it is because it is all about problems all teenagers face. Pregnancy is one of them.'

Of course, Mum had to be consulted, or in this case Frank's foster mother, Pippa, played by Vanessa Downing. She felt the subject was important, even if it was being raised at 6pm. 'Our characters deal with it in a more liberal way than some of the public might like, but I think that's a good thing. Kids are starting to have sex younger now, so it's a topic which shouldn't be avoided. Sex before marriage is up to the individual. Personally I think single-parenthood is a very bad thing, so the fact we're not promoting that is good … I think it's dealt with sensibly because we've let Frank and Roo make up their own minds. Even though I don't think marriage at that age is such a good thing, you have to let kids show their maturity if they have it.'

But there was one other problem and that was the baby itself. Abortion was ruled out by the producers and writers. They decided all to become midwives and attend the birth. But because this is a soap, the birth was not allowed to be easy. There was none of this waddling into a hospital one day and leaving a couple of days later carrying a baby. That wouldn't do at all. The birth had to be premature and the labour complicated.

Another problem arose. Justine wasn't exactly experienced in having babies. She'd been one herself only sixteen years previously. So, like any good actress, she did her research. 'I read a lot of books and watched

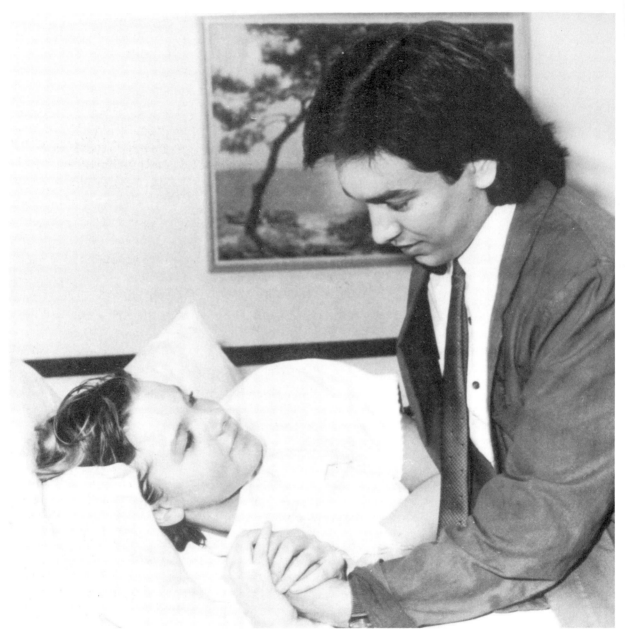

*Justine Clarke (Ruth) went to pre-natal classes to prepare for the fifteen scenes when her character was in labour. In the story Frank was there to hold Ruth's hand*

*The Fletcher 'parents'. In real life both Vanessa Downing
and Roger Oakley would consider adopting children*

*John Morris, who spent five months in the Summer Bay
community as Steven's uncle, Philip Matheson*

*A trio with complicated relationships – Ruth, Frank and Bobby
(Justine Clarke, Alex Papps and Nicolle Dickson)*

*Bobby – and two close screen friends.* Above right: *Alan Fletcher played by Simon Kay* and below right: *with Alex Papps*

*Justine Clarke, the glamorous Ruth Stewart and (right) Helena Bozich who plays Lynn Davenport*

*Alex Papps and Justine Clarke –*
*practising for a new career in music?*

*What does the future hold for Adam*
*Willits, now a veteran screen romeo?*

*John Farnham, known as 'Whispering Jack', who made a guest appearance on 'Home and Away'*

videos. But when it came down to it I still really wasn't prepared. I knew all about having a baby, but I didn't know what the physical pain was like. The wife of one of the directors had just had a baby and it was exactly the same situation. It was premature and there were complications. So I went out to her house and spent a lot of time with her. We'd do breathing exercises for two hours.'

The birth scenes involved a day's shooting for Justine. 'There were about fifteen scenes where I was actually in labour. I got a bit dizzy because I had to breathe so much. I started to hyperventilate. It was a long day.'

She was pleased the show didn't gloss over the pregnancy and instead showed it for the drama it was. 'It shows having a baby for someone so young isn't glamorous. But it was good for me as an actor and it was good for viewers of the show because it definitely wasn't an easy pregnancy and it wasn't an easy birth.'

One other thing the pregnancy did was to make her less a bitch in the eyes of the public. She doesn't hear the accusation of slut so much any more. 'A lot more people are coming up and saying hullo. I like that very much.'

# 7

## Sharyn Hodgson - Carly

Consider these incidents in the life and times of one character in 'Home and Away' as shown in the character synopsis: 'Tom and Pippa are distraught over Carly clearing out from home and heading into the city, where she feels new friends and the bright lights will help solve a multitude of problems and put her mind at ease. But she has fallen in with a bad crowd. ... Steve arrives in the city hoping to talk Carly into coming back home to the Fletcher household and is immediately alarmed to find how just how low some life is on the streets. He fears for Carly's safety. ... He pleads with her, and she makes a minor concession: "Alright, I really will try and get home for the Christmas Party." A dubious Steve departs the grim surroundings wondering if Carly will ever survive her new self-made hell-hole. The decorations are up and the guests start arriving at the Fletcher household. Soon everyone is into the festivities. Carly races towards Summer Bay in a taxi. At the caravan park she tells the cabbie to wait and slowly makes her way towards the house and the celebrations. She peers in, sees her family and friends enjoying the Christmas spirit. They're all so happy, so it seems. Guilt-ridden Carly heads back towards the taxi, unseen by the party-goers ...'

And you thought you had troubles. They are naught compared with what Carly Morris, the character played by Sharyn Hodgson, has gone through since 'Home and Away' first appeared on Australian television screens. She had her skull fractured when beaten up by her father, was raped while hitch-hiking, then got stuck heavily into the booze.

'Basically, Carly's a sad case the whole way through the show,' said Sharyn. 'The poor girl's demented, I swear, or at least she will be in a couple of years. She and I are so different – the way she thinks, everything. I feel sorry for her.'

Sharyn's upbringing contained nothing to prepare her for the trials and tribulations of being Carly. She lived in Panania, an anonymous suburb of brick houses with red tile roofs marching in orderly rows across the flat lands of Sydney's west. For one thing she lived a long way from the beach. For another her life before 'Home and Away' was, well, average would be the best description, even a little boring. Panania was not known for anything much except as the birth place of actor Bryan Brown and the Australian cricketing twins, Steve and Mark Waugh.

Her grandmother was an actress. 'She influenced me a lot while I was growing up – without me realising it,' she said. 'When I got into my teens I wanted to be a teacher but then it hit me that acting was what I wanted to do.'

After spending four years with the Phillip Street Drama School, studying every Saturday morning, she appeared in films produced by students with the Film and Television School. But apart from a small role in 'A Country Practice', she discovered that the path to her front door was not packed with agents and producers offering her work. So, after finishing school at eighteen, she worked in her father's business selling stationery and art supplies. It was not the world's most exciting job. She left and found employment with a newsagency. 'But on the day I was supposed to start I also got an audition for a job which was at the same time,' she said. 'I rang up the newsagency and told them I couldn't come in that day but then I won the audition and had to start straight away so I rang again and told them I couldn't take the job.'

Soon after she signed with 'Home and Away'. She was nineteen when she stepped into the shoes of Carly Morris. Seen by the writers this way: 'Carly has a vivacious personality, a quick mind and a distinct tendency to stretch the truth. She grew up adoring her mother and detesting her

*First kiss for Carly and Gary Samuels, played by Darius Perkins
(who played Scott Robinson in 'Neighbours' before Jason
Donovan took over the part)*

father (who owns and runs a very successful advertising agency). Her constant defiance of his authority infuriated him to the point where he started beating her. ... The death of her mother and a subsequent beating which left Carly with a fractured skull brought in the authorities. Despite the efforts of her father's lawyers to prevent it, Carly was taken away from him and fostered out to the Fletchers. She's adjusted well to living with Tom and Pippa. For the first time in her life her qualities are recognised and praised and it's like heaven to live in a family where the rights of the individual are respected. The scars are still there, but she's enjoying life too much to dwell on them.'

This was how Carly started life at Summer Bay. But she was soon in more hot water than a boiled egg. Her problems came about because, ignoring warnings, she began hitch-hiking here and there, doing what too many kids do, not only in Australia but around the world. You can see them lined up near any beach, trying to get a lift into the city, willing to ride with any stranger who pulls up and opens the car door. Some kids are never seen again.

The hitch-hiking scene caused considerable controversy. It showed Carly accepting a lift, then on her arrival home going straight to her room and bursting into tears. Not until the next day does she tell the other children she was attacked by the man who picked her up.

The word rape was never used. But the audience knew that more went on in the car than changing gears. There was some criticism that 6pm was too early a time to dramatise such sensitive subjects. Letters and telephone calls flooded into Channel Seven, in Sydney. The reactions were mixed, some congratulating the programme for warning kids of the dangers, others complaining such a frightening topic should not be exposed in such a timeslot.

In one way the hitch-hiking episode showed times have changed when it comes to certain subjects on television. For instance, the word condom would have raised sniggers had it been mentioned on television a few years ago. Now it's just another word in the English language.

'Five years ago condoms were not allowed to be mentioned on TV,' said Alan Bateman. 'AIDS had not arrived. It would have been a gratuitous issue to have a girl buying condoms on "A Country Practice" five years ago. It would have been an exploitive piece.'

Jim Davern, executive producer of 'A Country Practice', agreed. 'It's in the public interest to have one of our cast members going out and buying condoms. A few years ago you couldn't say pregnant on TV.'

Bateman fiercely defended the hitch-hiking scenes, emphasising that great care was taken with the storyline because of the early timeslot. 'It was never said Carly was raped nor were there any scenes of violence,' he said. 'It is an extremely sensitive issue in the community and it was vitally important we did not sensationalise it or trivialise it. Carly is a warm, nice character and to have something as dreadful as this happen to her, you have to be aware of the great affection viewers have for her character.' Bateman said teenagers in the age group of thirteen, fourteen and fifteen would be aware the term 'attacked' meant raped, but young children would relate the terminology to Stranger Danger, a campaign of education organised by the New South Wales Police Department. He added, 'I find the criticism very curious when on other channels you can be exposed to rape, murder and mayhem on the news'.

The scenes were not easy for Sharyn. She read everything available about attacks on hitch-hikers, tried to imagine herself in a similar position. She pictured the lonely road, the car stopping, the friendly driver suddenly turning vicious, then the humiliation and trauma of the violation. 'The more I read about it the more I realised that nobody is aware just how common it is,' she said. 'Attacks are happening every minute of the day in Sydney but a lot of them you never hear about.'

Having got that out of the way, Sharyn went head first into another incident in her character's complicated life. She had to get drunk. Well, personally she didn't have to get on the singing syrup, but she had to portray Carly with a bottle of sherry inside her. Again she found it difficult because she had never been drunk. She could not draw from real-life experience for help. 'I know people my age who drink, but luckily I don't know anyone who has a real alcohol problem. I most certainly don't.'

The storyline had Carly turning to drink instead of going to the local dance. After the attack while hitch-hiking, she doesn't want to be in the company of boys. She finds a bottle of sherry in the pantry and proceeds to get legless. 'In an earlier episode Carly tried some home brew and liked the feeling of being drunk,' said Sharyn. 'I guess that's what happens in real life as well. You try it once and think to yourself, "another time won't do any harm". I don't think my character drinking will encourage others because the message we're putting across is that alcohol is wrong. Most kids are going to try it at some stage of their lives and if they know what harm it can cause before they do it, then maybe it will discourage them. I really hope the episodes showed parents what kids can get up to with alcohol and show the kids who are doing it they can stop if they try.'

In comparison to the strife in which Carly finds herself, Sharyn lives a quiet life. Because of the long hours she finds little time for socialising. Her boyfriend works with the soap's crew and she sees him every day. But because she rarely goes out she has not been pestered by fans like

*Carly Morris (played by Sharyn Hodgson) finds peace and security with the Fletchers after her violent childhood. But after an even more violent encounter while hitch-hiking she turns to drink ...*

other cast members. 'Now and then people ask me for my autograph and it's really embarrassing,' she said. 'I'm rarely out on the streets for people to recognise me but when they do it's a weird feeling.'

She is down to earth. She considers her position and shakes her head. 'Acting is definitely not a glamorous job. All I see it as is becoming someone else when you're not being yourself.'

She sees a life beyond acting. 'One day I'd like to study archaeology. It has always been in the back of my mind. I'd love to discover ancient ruins. It would be great to dig a hole, find a trapdoor, open it up and find the rest of Rome.'

If she succeeds she might find herself in familiar territory. Ancient Rome was, after all, little more than a soap opera on a grand scale.

# Nicolle Dickson – Nothing Like Bobby

In the far western suburbs of Sydney, a long, long way from the beaches and a million miles from Summer Bay, there is a garage. It is a perfectly ordinary garage in a perfectly ordinary backyard in a suburb that wears its ordinariness like a badge of honour. This is working-class Sydney. All pretentiousness stops here. Should you be invited inside the garage you will find it occupied by a nineteen-year-old with urchin looks and a wicked laugh. She might be wearing something outrageous bought for a few dollars from a secondhand clothing shop.

The garage is the home of Nicolle Dickson, who plays the streetwise delinquent, Bobby Simpson. 'I thought about leaving home,' she said. 'I started to get restless and I wanted to move out of home and do my own thing, be my own person. But then I realised there isn't any pressure at home. You don't have to put up any fronts. So here I am, living in the garage. My grandfather used to be in there, too, so it's all decorated. And I've got a futon bed.'

She has a darkroom set up in the bedroom so she can follow her passion for photography. She was going to be a photographer, studied the subject at the Sydney School of Arts, where she undertook a Bachelor of Visual Arts, but somewhere along the way she was diverted into acting.

All this may sound unimportant, the sort of gossip vital only to fan magazines, but it holds clues to Nicolle's personality. She spends a lot of time in the garage and the darkroom because she is a private person, the attention she receives from fans is something she finds difficulty in coping with.

She likes walking in the neighbourhood. The problem is kids she has never seen before whistle and shout at her and call, 'Hi, Bobby!'

She cringes. 'I don't feel comfortable with that aspect of the fame – these people don't even know my real name. I never thought people would recognise me when I was out in public. I thought that because I'm so short and wear glasses, nobody would notice me.'

Notice her? Because of the popularity of 'Home and Away' she stands out like a giant at a midgets' convention. Sometimes fans come up to her and shove pieces of paper under her nose. They do it without saying a word. Just the piece of paper and a grunt. She worries about that. 'I don't mind when people ask me to sign my name. After all, it's not much to ask, is it? But sometimes they don't say much to me at all. I think they're scared to talk to me because they think I'm going to bite their head off.'

They didn't teach her about fame at drama school. It wasn't on the curriculum. Nicolle knew she had to cope with it herself, and it wasn't easy, not when you're a private person and perhaps a little suspicious of strangers. 'It seems strange people want to make a fuss over you when you're only doing your job. People feel they have to be attached to this "star" image. I suppose that everyone really wants to be a success, or be connected with success somehow, and this is just a more public and more obvious way of showing it.'

Nicolle, it must be understood, doesn't see herself as a star. To her stars are the big names on the cinema screen. Robert Redford is a star and so is Meryl Streep, not nineteen-year-old girls from working class suburbs of Sydney. 'I always think of a star as someone like Laurence Olivier. When people say I'm a star I say, "No I'm not, I'm an actor." I live in the western suburbs. I like going out for walks all the time by myself. Maybe if I wear my hair differently people won't recognise me.'

Oddly enough, Nicolle found a kind of anonymity in going to hear bands at nightclubs. No one bothered her. 'The people there either don't know much about me being in "Home and Away" or they just don't care.'

*They didn't teach Nicolle Dickson about fame at drama school –
but now, recognised as Bobby Simpson wherever she goes, she
is learning to live with it*

Nicolle hasn't been around much. Before she signed with 'Home and Away' she had never been out of Sydney or flown on an aircraft, unusual for an Australian teenager, most of whom have scuttled about like tour guides before even leaving school. Suddenly she was thrust into a world of first-class service, limousines taking her here and there, aircraft whisking her around Australia for promotional appearances.

At first she resented it. 'This is taking me away from my private life and I'm not seeing my friends,' she said one day.

After a while she decided she might as well lie back and enjoy it. 'There are plenty of other actors out of work who can't afford these luxuries,' she said.

One of the little luxuries was her own bodyguard. All the cast of 'Home and Away' have bodyguards when they visit shopping centres around the country, members of a Sydney security company called Blue Falcons. They are experts in self-defence; some have earned a blackbelt in karate, others are or were exponents of the boxing ring and their job is to ensure the fans do not touch the actors. 'Every move is planned ahead to get the actors in and out of these public arenas without hassle and harrassment,' said Gary Farrar, a publicist for Channel Seven, Sydney, who liaises with cast and security. 'The big thing for fans is, of course, to touch the actors – which is what we try to prevent. Because once they start touching, they start ripping. A lot of them [the bodyguards] are good-looking guys, but guys who can speak well, are approachable and can maintain law and order whenever necessary. There's usually one man in the group who is large and bulky, with hands the size of an elephant's foot. People soon get the message that these fellows mean business. Of course we don't have guys with scars and tattoos. We don't want to scare people away. And it's no use having bodyguards who are small because the odd – pardon the expression – smartarse in the crowd would only have a field day.'

Nicolle soon discovered that appearing in a soap involved more than learning lines and emoting for the benefit of the cameras. Appearing in a soap included such mundane and time-consuming tasks as answering fanmail when the body is tired, the mind edgy, the only desire to stretch out and sleep. 'Every time Bobby punches someone I get heaps of letters.'

She admits there are times when the pressures get too much. Then she does what any sensible teenage girl does. 'I just have to go to my parents and cry about it. They're really understanding.'

In other words, Nicolle is nothing like her character. Nothing. According to the writers, Bobby Simpson is 'Summer Bay's premiere juvenile delinquent – the product of sixteen years of emotional rejection by her parents, and later, grandparents. A loner, the only person she confided in prior to the arrival of Tom and Pippa was Ailsa Hogan. She has a few mates, basically the more tearaway kids in town. By the time Bobby was twelve she had managed to polarise the attitude of the town towards her. If she liked you she'd do anything for you, if she had an anti against you she was a little demon who'd only stop short of crime in her actions towards you. The pro Bobby faction is led by the kind-hearted Ailsa, the anti by the devious deputy headmaster, Donald Fisher. The Fletchers find themselves in conflict with Fisher as they try to help the alienated young girl.'

There are times when Nicolle dislikes Bobby, disagrees with the actions the character takes. 'When Bobby turned her back on her foster parents to go off and look for her real father, I just became totally frustrated with her. Part of her popularity is because she does all the things other people wish they were brave enough to do. She'll stick by you to the end, but then she can turn around and stick her fingers up at you if she doesn't like you. I think a lot of people can relate to the way Bobby is. But, yes, I enjoy playing her. I think she's really sweet because she puts on this tough exterior and yet inside she's longing for somebody. Bobby has a little control over the others and that's interesting to play.'

In her early years Nicolle wasn't afire with ambition to be an actress. All she wanted was to attend drama and dancing classes with her younger sister. In fact, she wasn't sure if she wanted to be anything at all after she and her sister were involved in a bad car accident. Nicolle received a broken jaw, but the worst damage was to her self-esteem. She lost all motivation, felt responsible for the crash and the terrifying experience she had put her sister through. But with support from her family and friends she tested for the role of Bobby.

'Getting the part did wonders for my self-confidence,' she said. 'I went through a very bad stage. I was really depressed. I was only eighteen, but I thought, "Oh, no, I'm going to give up." You take it so personally.'

She put the accident from her mind as work took over and she travelled from location to location, including Palm Beach. The cast once had rosy visions about filming on Palm Beach, of hot sun and balmy breezes, of golden sands and warm seas. And furthermore they were being paid for the pleasure. They forgot that Sydney has a winter when the wind is edged with ice and the temperature drops below 50 degrees. Taping doesn't stop because of the seasons. The cast has to act like the temperature was over the century mark.

Simon Kay, a guest actor in the soap, recalled the day when the wind, bitingly cold, was so strong it caused havoc with the equipment. It was his first day on 'Home and Away' and he was called upon to dive enthusiastically into the ocean. 'It was absolute hell,' he said. 'I had to be up at 5am and into a wetsuit in order to be at the beach by 6am. It was freezing, and I had to carry this surfboard down to the water, forcing my way against the wind. It was so bad the crew had a difficult time trying to cover and protect the boom – and this was supposed to be happening during an Australian summer. I had cut my heel open on the fin of the surfboard, but because I was so numb I didn't know about it until someone pointed out the blood in the sand. The coldest part was the sand; it made me ache. The water was the warmest spot, so I did a very gung-ho thing and just dived in ...'

Besides the dubious delights of Palm Beach in winter, Nicolle found she spent a lot of time in the Green Room at Channel Seven, along with the other young actors slumped wearily waiting for their next scene. They have been working six days a week. They rest when and where they can, sometimes dropping to sleep in the make-up department where a photograph of Alex Papps has been glued to the wall next to a picture of a deranged-looking man covered in pimples. 'Alex Papps before and after make-up,' the caption reads.

Maybe she has to cry in the next scene. There is a great deal of crying in soaps. In fact there is more crying than laughing, the actors expected to turn on the tears like they had taps in their heads. They might not be tested for their crying ability at auditions but a quick flick through their scripts shows that tears are as important to soaps as a lack of them is to westerns. Nicolle admits to being reasonably adept at crying. 'I cry on

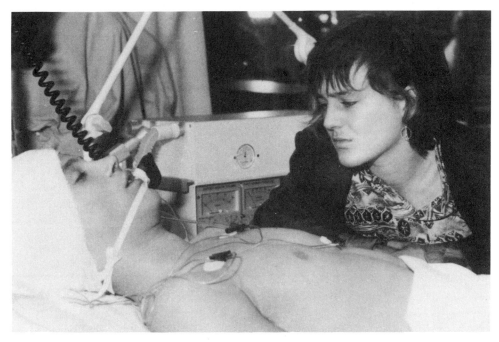

*Bobby, former juvenile delinquent, shows her sensitive side at*
*the bedside of Alan Fisher (played by Simon Kay), only son of*
*the man who loathes her*

camera the same way I do at home. I just have a big build-up where I
hold everything in, then I let it go. I do all this heavy panting and stuff. I
can't even speak when I cry because I'm getting so emotional.'

Much of the crying came about because her character was in love
with Frank, but had to take a back seat to Roo for a while. The situation
was cleared up, as they always are in soaps, and Bobby and Frank were
allowed to get on with their romance. The writers thought, why not
another wedding?

But would the audience like it? Alex and Nicolle were on display at a
shopping centre when he gave her a hearty hug. The crowd went wild.

'Let's have a scream from those who want Bobby and Frank to
marry,' Alex shouted.

The crowd went berserk. The public might not have arranged the
marriage but it heartily approved of the idea. And what the public wants
the public gets. It has always been so in soaps.

# Adam Willits' First Screen Kiss

Tom Cruise is a heart-throb – that is, a youngish actor of the male species who has the ability to make teenage girls weak at the knees and their mothers weak in the head. Johnny Depp is one and Michael J. Fox another. And there's Adam Willits.

Adam Willits? Yes, that's the name!

Furthermore, he is a mere sixteen years old. He plays Steve Matheson in 'Home and Away' and those who concern themselves with such matters as heart-throbs suggest he is well on the way to joining that select circle. He could be the youngest heart-throb in history, or at least since Romeo caused Juliet's heart to flutter.

Besides looking good, a heart-throb must be able to appear in romantic scenes for the benefit of the cameras, must be able to open the lips and indulge in passionate kisses without turning the colour of an extremely ripe tomato. Adam has accomplished this without too much bother. 'But they've been old women – women in their twenties,' he said of his screen partners. He was only half joking.

Adam was not inexperienced in acting when he signed for 'Home and Away'. In fact, he had an agent when he was nine and was working in productions by amateur musical societies. By the time he was twelve he had appeared in the feature film, *Marbles*, for the Australian Film and Television School and the play, 'All My Sons', for the Ensemble Theatre. Later he appeared in the feature films, *Anna, Damsels be Damned, Weekend of the Lonesome Rustler* and *Mad Max III*, and the television movie, *The Perfectionist.*

To most kids, Adam's early life seems ideal. He was being paid good money for playing games, albeit for the cameras. But as he looks back over his handful of years, Adam is not so sure. 'If someone made me unknown tomorrow and said, "Okay, let's start again", I would quite happily go back to school and take it from there. It's been a long haul to get this far, and although I'm enjoying what I'm doing now, I would never be a child actor again.'

His character is described by the writers this way: 'Steven, sixteen, is quiet and studious with an inventive mind. From the word go he had a charmed life, blessed with loving, caring parents. Everything was perfect in his life until the night of 10th June 1987. His mate Danny, who lived across the road, had invited him to stay over for the night. Steven did so. He awoke at two in the morning to the sounds of fire engines. To his horror he saw his house ablaze – his parents trapped in the fire. But he had more than the death of his parents to overcome – he had no extended family to care for him. The [welfare] department put Steve in a home briefly until they could place him with a suitable family. Thus he came to Tom and Pippa's – a disturbed boy who still had terrible nightmares about his parents' deaths. Basically, Steve is a good kid. He has the potential to be a wonderful human being or a pompous brat. Tom and Pippa become concerned as time goes by to see him tending towards the latter. They are going to have to fight to keep this nice kid nice.'

Adam leapt into his role with enthusiasm, even if it did mean he had no spare time for the things he liked such as soccer and listening to bands. When he wasn't working in the soap, he was doing his school years 11 and 12 by correspondence. He wasn't even sure about his character. 'I don't relate to Steven at all,' he said. 'I love to get out of his character when the shooting is finished, and to ruffle up my hair which is all brushed like Steven's. It's really hard to get involved with his character on set, because he is so different to me.'

But he did enjoy kissing. One day he was told he was about to have his first screen kiss. He couldn't wait to get his hands on the script. Flipping through the pages he ticked off his kissing scenes. 'Three ... four ... five ... six ... seven,' he murmured.

'But we kissed a lot more than that,' he said later. 'When you consider rehearsals and retakes, we kissed a hell of a lot. It was great.'

He quickly became something of an expert on kissing, helped by his screen partner, Amanda Newman-Phillips, who played Narelle. Amanda was twenty-three. Apparently there is more to kissing than meets the eye, or for that matter, the lips.

'She gave me all the pointers,' he told *TV Week's* Leigh Reinhold, 'like coming in at the right angle so our noses don't touch, not to close my eyes, not to pucker.'

He explained how his character got involved in such an interesting situation. 'It's not as if we are in love. It's more physical. I've got this plan that I can get her to kiss me, because I've done a survey and I'm a pretty hot kisser. It starts out she's trying to teach me to kiss, then we get involved.'

Amanda didn't mind at all planting a few on Adam's lips, even though

*Sixteen-year-old Steven Matheson (played by Adam Willits) grows up quickly during the series – both as best man and screen lover*

it was her first screen kiss. 'Adam's a sweetie,' she said. 'After all the fuss had died down it was great fun.'

Studying Adam's performance and that of Alex Papps, noting that in the heart-throb business the younger end of the audience was well catered for, Alan Bateman decided some fine tuning was necessary. He knew the soap was attracting viewers up to eighteen and over forty. What was needed was 'hunk value', as they say in the trade, to appeal to women between about twenty and forty. A few emotional wallops, Bateman reasoned, wouldn't go astray.

Enter John Morris, twenty-five, a former soldier from Perth. But he didn't enter easily; in fact, he almost didn't enter at all. Not long after arriving in Sydney from the other side of the continent, John was about to get out of a train at one of the stations on the Sydney underground system when his leg caught in the train door. The train moved, dragging John along the platform, bouncing him over the concrete, scraping away skin. He could see the tunnel archway getting closer, the wheels beneath him, and he knew he had only a few seconds to live. At the last moment, at that split second when he wondered how his obituary would read, he managed to kick himself free.

'After that train business – which was pretty heavy, let me tell you, it completely freaked me out – I knew my luck could only change for the better,' he said.

Along with 150 actors, he auditioned for the part of Dr Philip Matheson, who goes to Summer Bay to check up on his nephew, Steven, and decides to stay on. He got the role.

'I'm just rapt in the opportunity I've been given,' he said at the time, 'because apart from several little bits and pieces, my television experience is nil. Now I've landed a big role like this. I feel very proud of myself – and not a little humble – to think that out of 150 actors from Melbourne to Sydney they gave the part to me.'

He moved into Summer Bay in June 1988. Five months later he moved out, never to be seen again.

The reason given by both sides was that the character was not working out as well as it should. In other words, some heart-throbs make it, others don't. And no one really knows why. If they knew the formula they would bottle it and sell it.

Two other young men call Summer Bay home. They were there from the beginning. Neither could be called heart-throbs. They could be called many things, including yobbos and larrikans, but not even their closest friends would suggest they are in the business of making female hearts throb.

It is nothing to do with the actors, Peter Vroom and Craig Thompson, but with the characters they play, Lance Smart and Martin Dibble. Says their characters' biography: 'Lance and Martin work at the local oyster farm which is run by the brother of Donald Fisher, the deputy headmaster at Summer Bay. A couple of local yobbos, they have harboured a grudge against Fisher since he had them drummed out of the school cadet corps. Their great nemesis in life is the local surfies who get all the girls. The boys can't understand why they don't. After all, Martin believes he's the most irresistible male in Summer Bay and Lance, always greatly impressed by Martin, can only agree.'

Neither had appeared on television before signing with 'Home and Away'. Peter Vroom, nineteen, did a variety of jobs before leaving school in 1984, including one as a motor mechanic and a deckhand on a ferry.

Craig Thompson, twenty, helped pay for acting lessons by working as an apprentice greenkeeper for two years, on garbage trucks and as a labourer. He was an amateur boxer for three years.

While they have nothing against their characters, in fact, the opposite, they get a trifle annoyed that the public expect them to be dummies and yobbos twenty-four hours a day.

Said Craig, 'You have to keep yourself in control and be nice when people approach you. If you snub them sooner or later it will come back on you.'

'Most people are great,' added Peter. 'What I hate about all this is that people who put themselves out of my league before are suddenly coming up to me and being nice.'

Peter sometimes yearns to get into what he called 'more proper' acting. 'Every now and again we have a really serious, good scene and I enjoy doing it,' he said. 'But I like comedy too.'

Craig agrees. 'I like doing comedy. Martin and Lance are very different roles from the rest of the cast, so they tend to stand out a lot. They're just, well, OTT – over the top.'

*Peter Vroom (who plays Lance Smart) and Craig Thomson (who plays Martin Dibble) are sometimes irritated when they're expected to be yobbos in real life*

But occasionally they wonder not only about their characters but the others played by younger actors. The characters are censored, or to be more accurate what comes out of their mouths is subject to a heavy blue pencil. A 6pm timeslot does not allow kids to act and talk entirely as they might in real life. One could argue that even a midnight timeslot would be too early to put on the screen what teenagers do and say when not in the company of their parents.

'Lance and Martin are definitely drinkers,' said Peter, 'and if it wasn't for the timeslot they would be into marijuana too. Critics did slam the show for lack of realism in the characters, but you have to be a bit responsible with so many kids watching. Lance and Martin can't swear either, although I don't know why they change the scripts because the average fifteen-year-old swears like a trooper.'

# 10

# The Fishers and the Fletchers

Norman Coburn was sitting quietly on the bus taking him to his home in Bondi, reading a newspaper, minding his business, bothering no one. Something distracted his attention. Glancing up, he saw a sturdy young lad glaring at him in the manner of a landlady examining the sheets of a departed guest.

Then the lad plonked himself on the seat beside Norman. Oh, no, thought Norman, this is it. I'm going to get it for being such a bastard to the kids in 'Home and Away'.

And he is a bastard, if you'll excuse the language, to the younger population of Summer Bay. His character, Donald Fisher, the deputy headmaster of the local school, is the sort of teacher to whom one would give an apple only if it were rotten. There's one in every school.

The writers make it clear Fisher is an unlovely person: 'There is no love lost between the Fishers and the Fletchers – his victimisation of Bobby caused ill-feeling between them from the day the Fletchers moved into Summer Bay. Fisher knows he is not liked in the community … but feels he's done a lot for the town and received very little in return. He sees himself as a decent man of strong principle and to a point that's right. The problem is that Fisher is incapable of seeing the harm his narrow-minded attitudes can do.'

So there he was, this hugely unliked figure being scrutinised closely by a glowering young lad on the 380 bus to Bondi. It was not a little unnerving. After a while the lad spoke.

'Do you live in a mansion?' he muttered. And that was all he said.

Norman was relieved. As he said later, 'I was expecting a good dressing down. But the lad's prime concern was not so much the character but the fact he presumed all actors lived in mansions.'

He doesn't live in a mansion. His abode is much more humble because he has been one of those actors who was never a big star but without whom theatre and television drama could not exist. Working in theatre and radio when he was fourteen, he joined the Elizabethan Theatre Trust when it was formed in the mid-fifties and spent two years with the company touring Australia in plays. In those years opportunities for actors in Australia were not so much lean as practically non-existent. As did many actors, Norman headed to England where he worked on weekly repertory throughout Britain. He also did television work, popping up in such popular shows as 'Coronation Street', 'The Professionals' and 'No Hiding Place'.

'Home and Away' brings back memories of his repertory days. The pay might be better now, the conditions superior and he is not required to return each night to lodgings run by retired chorus girls with a love of the gin bottle and a hatred of changing the bedclothes – but there remains a similarity between the two. Repertory was the training ground of actors. Now soaps have taken over the role.

'In the theatre I rehearsed all day the play for the following week, but would also be playing in the play we rehearsed the week before,' he said. 'One's entire life was spent in the pocket of a company of about ten or twelve people, and that's how you learned the job. The difference now is the horrendous situation where each night you might be seen by millions of viewers rather than thirty or forty in an audience. And on television you don't get the time to explore a character like you would in weekly stage shows. I was probably dreadful in 90 per cent of the parts I played in repertory theatre. But having done that, when it comes to playing a character on television, I can draw different facets of the character because I've played them before.'

He is refreshingly frank about his first weeks in 'Home and Away',

*The man everybody loves to hate: Norman Coburn who plays
deputy headmaster Donald Fisher*

for tucked away in all that vast experience was the curious belief that all
acting was the same, whether it be on stage or television. 'I don't think
that is true now,' he said. 'On television you have to do less externally
and concentrate more inwardly. I don't think I was very good when I
started to play Fisher. I don't like watching myself but I looked at the
show a couple of times and it was too big – the character was all over the
place. Hopefully now I've been able to bring it down to someone's nine-
inch screen and still retain the energy.'

His one regret is the death of his son, or rather Fisher's son, Alan. For the sake of dramatic content, the writers decided that Fisher junior, a confused adolescent who wanted nothing more than the love and respect of his father, should be sent to his final audition in the sky. He died from a terminal illness, but not before having a brief fling with Bobby Simpson.

*Simon Kay, who played Alan, Mr Fisher's son. In the series Alan dies of a terminal illness; only time will tell if the show's producers can perform a miracle and bring him back to life*

The character was played by Simon Kay, twenty-one, not only a fine actor but a man with the sort of good looks that would gain him entry to the heart-throb department.

'I am sorry they killed him off,' said Norman. 'Simon is a damned fine little actor and it would have been an advantage having him around. I'm sure the producers and writers now regret his demise very much as well. But what can they do? They can't very well bring him back.'

Or can they? Realising their mistake, the producers did think of ways to resurrect him from the dead, to make him the new Lazarus. Other soaps that made the same mistake, that is, killed off characters too soon, have had few qualms about playing God and doing the impossible. Probably the greatest resurrection in the history of soaps was performed by Bobby Ewing, of 'Dallas', who returned from the dead after being killed in a car smash. Sometimes the character has returned as a twin. Anything is possible in soaps. The writers of 'Home and Away' spent considerable time thinking about Simon's character and at one stage came up with a fiendishly complex suggestion.

Explained Simon, 'The suggestion was that Alan's father writes a book and it was thought a film should be made of the book which told all about Alan's untimely death. There would be a search for an actor to play Alan in the movie … and all of a sudden this young man with a moustache or whatever happens to come along and he's a dead ringer for Alan. And guess who was going to play this man? I would certainly love to go back into "Home and Away". But I would have to have some very serious talks with the producers beforehand.'

Norman Coburn was one of eight older actors who signed originally for 'Home and Away', if only to show the world is not entirely populated by people under the age of twenty. There have to be parents, schoolteachers, shopkeepers and bosses. Someone has to keep the kids under control. Someone has to pay the rent.

Ray Meagher is one of the oldies. He plays Alf Stewart, described as a 'good-natured rogue with a finger in every pie. By the age of thirty Alf owned the Summer Bay Liquor Store, the boat hire service, the Summer Bay Caravan Park and a yacht brokerage. Married to a local lass whom he adored, he was shattered by her death from drowning in 1985. They lived at what is now the Fletcher house. After her death, he could no

*Alan (Simon Kay) tells his father Donald Fisher a few home*
*truths about his relationship with Bobby*

longer stand living there ... but kept the house spick and span while
letting the caravan park slide into the state of disrepair it is in when
bought by the Fletchers. When Ailsa Hogan came to town he went
courting again. He is very attracted to Ailsa but is still unsure how far he
wants the relationship to go. A relationship that is strained by the hostility
of Ruth (his only child) towards Ailsa.'

Ray Meagher's face was well known before he took up residence in
Summer Bay. Everyone knew the face but few could put a name to it
because in sixty television productions, twenty-nine films and twenty
stage shows he has played characters – colourful, offbeat, at times
downright nasty characters, and each portrayed so skilfully the actor was
lost behind the mask. 'I've played some very important supporting roles
but character actors are not promoted in Australia,' he said. 'It never
really annoys me. It's something you just accept as an actor.'

At least he is not short of roles. Beginning work in the noble business
of calling horse races in Queensland, he has been seen as a grotty horse
thief, a charming bum, a back-slapping bore, a cynical newspaper editor

and a tough, ambitious cop. Among his movie successes was *Breaker Morant*. In 1988, a year many actors cursed as one where work was as scarce as water in the Sahara and thirsted for money as a result, he was in three mini series – *The Shiralee, True Believers* and *Spit MacPhee.*

'I've never had a burning desire to play any character in particular,' he said. 'It's just a matter of having a look at a script and making a decision whether I want to play a part or not. I really see acting as a business. It's nice when you get a role which is artistically and financially good. But sometimes decisions are made purely on an artistic level and at other times on a business level.'

'Home and Away' is his first regular soapie and the character of Alf Stewart is a change of pace. 'It's good for me to play someone like that after all the other blokes,' he said. 'And working with the likes of Judy Nunn and Fiona Spence and so on, is terrific. We have a lot of fun between ourselves, let me tell you. There is never a dull moment.'

One would have to be an extremely glum person not to have fun when Judy Nunn is around. A talented actress and writer, she is given to doing the unexpected and outrageous statements are expected to fall from her lips like jokes from a comedian on a talk show.

At Melbourne Airport a few years ago the businessmen and others waiting for their invariably delayed aircraft to Sydney were sitting in the bar drinking and grumbling. In walked a woman who turned all heads at once, like the laughing clown heads at a carnival. She was wearing a leotard cut to her waist, black fishnet stockings, Marilyn Monroe-styled shoes, blonde wig and false eyelashes. Over this garish costume was a short leather coat incapable of hiding much, especially when the woman sat down. The guys in the bar watched with increasing interest; this was better than sitting around complaining about delayed aircraft.

'I was playing a sex-bomb, a magician's assistant for the television series, "Holiday Island",' said Judy. 'I wore the costume from Melbourne to Sydney as a dare. Then the plane was delayed and I had to sit in the bar for an hour with men trying to pick me up.' Then there was her statement about marriage. 'I don't believe in marriage as an institution. I don't believe in the pressures it places on two people. My parents have had an extremely happy marriage for many years. As for me, I believe totally in relationships but I don't believe in sticking together if you are unhappy ... If a man isn't making me happy I'll shoot through and find one that does. I'm a positive thinker and remove things that upset me ...'

The years passed. Times changed. In 1988 Judy was married twice in one week.

The first occasion was for the benefit of her character, described this way: 'Ailsa has only been at Summer Bay for a year, but the locals were quick to accept her as one of the community. Warm-hearted and generous to a fault, she is a sucker for anyone who isn't given a fair go – hence her staunch defence of Bobby. Ailsa runs the local grocery store. When we meet her she's in a relationship with Alf Stewart and has a wide circle of friends in Summer Bay. She seems like the kind of woman whose life is an open book. But Ailsa has a past she's very anxious to keep secret.'

*Ailsa Hogan (played by Judy Nunn) and Alf Stewart (Ray Meagher) have a close relationship on the set – and a lot of laughs off it*

In no time at all the writers had Ailsa and Alf tying the knot. They did it secretly, surprising their friends in Summer Bay with the announcement they were now man and wife.

As the scenes were being shot, Judy was planning her own wedding for the following Saturday to a former Hong Kong and Australian cop, Bruce Venables.

The wedding day drew closer. Judy kept looking at the sky because downpours over the previous two weeks had disrupted production. If there was any more rain she might have to work on her wedding day.

'It's a bit tense,' she said, a couple of days before her own ceremony. 'But I'm more worried about it raining on the wedding day because we're having the ceremony in our back garden. Still, I suppose we could use a marquee – or as another contingency plan I could slit my wrists.'

The marriage went ahead without the need of a marquee or the spilling of blood. 'Getting married is a good thing to do, actually,' she said. 'It's chaotic trying to organise it when you're working but it was all worth the trouble. Towards the end I had been thinking, "I can't do this and work at the same time" and was wondering why we didn't just run off to a registry office like Ailsa and Alf. But now I'm glad we didn't.'

The history of Australian soaps could not be written without mentioning Judy Nunn. Her first professional job was at the age of twelve at the Perth Playhouse. She came to Sydney when she was nineteen, stayed for three years and went to England where she worked for six years in repertory, radio and television alongside such notable performers as John Gregson, Wilfred Pickles, Jessi Mathews and Julia Lockwood.

Her first role was in 'The Box', one of the earliest Australian soaps, in which she played the extremely bitchy Vicki Stafford. 'I only wanted a three-month contract with "The Box," she said. 'But I ended up playing Vicki for three-and-a-half years. In television, typecasting comes easily ...'

Her next soap was 'Skyways', set around an airport. 'The episodes are knockouts,' she declared at the time. 'In soap opera one is prepared to merely grab the money and run. But this one was so wonderful to work on. There I am in some lovely little plane from some air museum, wearing a Biggles helmet and flying gear.'

Unfortunately, the public wasn't as enthusiastic about 'Skyways' as Judy. It lasted only a few months. She appeared next in 'Prisoner' followed by 'A Country Practice' and 'Sons and Daughters'. When she wasn't appearing in soaps, she was writing them, doing scripts for 'Neighbours' and 'Possession', as well as writing children's books and plays.

'Writing is a lonely business for anybody but for me it was particularly lonely because most of my working life has been spent as an actress,' she said. 'Suddenly I spent a year locked up with a computer ... I just wish I could be back in a nice comfortable safe soap.'

She got her wish when she was signed to 'Home and Away'. She has no prejudice against soaps, in fact is scornful of those actors who declare they would not be seen dead in one. Soaps cause that reaction. Few people admit to watching them and few actors would cheerfully confess they would give an arm and a leg to be working regularly in them.

However, in the Eighties most actors have changed their minds. They have little choice; these days in the Australian entertainment industry if they don't work in soaps they could find themselves queuing at the dole office.

'All that stigma business has vanished now,' said Judy. 'Now, every well-known actor around town will say, "A year in a soap? Okay." Then they get a bit bored and then they say, "Oh, the scripts are ratshit" and things like that. But in the meantime, that'll buy them their house, won't it? No, we don't sneer at that any more ... It's a dog-eat-dog world and we've all got to survive.'

Judy has survived well. So has Fiona Spence, who plays Celia Stewart, described this way by the writers: 'Celia is Alf's youngest sister, one of the four girls in the family. She is the town's busy-body spinster, bitter that love has passed her by and taking that bitterness out on the world. ... Celia is a major ally of the bigoted Fisher. She loves a gossip – it helps fill her life. But given that, there is not a malicious bone in her body.'

What Fiona survived was three years being known as Vinegar Tits. She earned the title in the soap, 'Prisoner', when she played Vera Bennet, the tough, sour-faced and thoroughly despised prison wardress. Audiences loved to loathe the severe, sad creature with her hair in a butch bun and a face that carried a perpetual sneer.

'Celia is so different; she's very vulnerable, unlike Vera,' said Fiona.

'That doesn't mean to say I didn't enjoy playing Vera. I did – very much. She was very important to me for a long, long time. I could not have wished to play a better character in my first major television role.

Unlike most of the cast of 'Home and Away', who seemed to start in show business not long after they learned to walk, Fiona didn't begin an acting career until she was twenty-seven. After leaving school she did 'the obligatory secretarial course': which took her to Montreal for the Australian Pavilion at the Canadian Expo. She spent a year there, then headed to London. When she returned to Australia she worked in the travel industry for three years, before once again departing for London. Finally she decided to call Australia home and joined the Independent Theatre School.

After a year in 'Home and Away', Fiona hoped her character would change a little. Find a guy, perhaps dress up. Fiona thought it wouldn't be bad at all if she was allowed to wear outfits that had a touch of glamour. After all, she was three years in a prison wardress's uniform. So she was more than a little pleased when the writers hinted her character could be spruced up. 'There's a touch of romance that will be wonderful for Celia,' she said. 'And there will be a remarkable change in her appearance. Celia will be going on a shopping spree to buy some rather smart outfits. Wait until you see her.'

Perhaps the most important of the oldies, as far as the writers are concerned, is the character of Tom Fletcher, played by Roger Oakley. According to the writers, 'Forty-year-old Tom is an idealist and a dreamer – a gentle man with a creative mind. He comes from a broken home himself. His father shot through when he was born, his mother decided to foster him out when he was two years old and he's never seen her since. He and Pippa have been married for ten years and are very much in love. When it looked like they couldn't have a family of their own he suggested they become foster parents. Because Pippa realised it was Tom's background that made him try and provide a good home for some of the rejects – kids other people wouldn't touch with a barge pole – she agreed. They applied for their first child and it's a decision Tom has never regretted.'

When executive producer, Alan Bateman, announced the cast for 'Home and Away' he said of Roger: 'He is so good on the screen, when

*New Zealand-born Roger Oakley, who plays Tom Fletcher is a veteran actor with many Australian film and television credits to his name. He has considered adopting children in real life*

people see him they will be asking where has he been all their lives.'

Roger's whereabouts was not a mystery. The New Zealand-born actor came to Australia in 1978 and appeared in 'The Sullivans', an extremely successful soap set in the period of the Second World War. He followed that with roles in the television productions 'Against The Wind', 'Eureka Stockade', 'Sara Dane', 'Women of the Sun' and 'Carson's Law' and films 'Ground Zero', 'Travelling North' and 'Sleeping Dogs'. 'Working on "Home and Away" is the longest I've ever worked in one stretch,' he said. 'It's what they call a break, isn't it? It shows it can happen to anyone. I feel also that, in a sense, it's my turn. I've served my time.'

Since playing the role of a foster parent, Roger has thought about the subject. A bachelor in his early forties, he believes that if he does not marry he would rather foster a child than became an actual parent.

'I've only thought vaguely about whether or not I'd ever have a family because I haven't been close enough to a lady to think, "Well, this is going to be it." It's the way my life has gone,' he told *TV Week*.

'Unless you've been very close to a partner, I suppose you can't really know how you'd feel if you were in that situation. But I think it would be nice if people would relax and get off focusing on having their own kids and get on with looking after the kids who are already here – and there are plenty here.

'I can understand a married couple wanting to have a child of their own because to have kids is our biological urge. But now that I'm a little bit older I talk to women who say they would still like to have a family or, for reasons, can't have a family and I think, even with In-Vitro fertilisation and so on, which is exciting, for them to foster a child would be a terrific thing to do and we'd all be better off. To me, fostering a child would be just as acceptable as having a child of my own, but obviously it would have to be just as acceptable to the other half.'

# 11

---

# The McPhees

---

Sheila Kennelly was in a quandary. As far as quandaries go, it was not unpleasant because it involved a choice of jobs, a situation rare among those who seek to make a living out of acting. Her choice was between a movie and a soapie, between a single pay packet and one, hopefully, each week.

The problem was the movie was perhaps the most important to be shot in Australia in the past two or three years. Called *Evil Angels,* it told the story of Michael Chamberlain, a Seventh Day Adventist pastor, and his wife Lindy, whose six-week-old child, Azaria, disappeared one cold night from Ayers Rock, in the dead centre of Australia, in 1980. Lindy said a dingo, a wild Australian dog, took her baby. The police thought otherwise and charged her with murder. She was sentenced to life imprisonment but a commission of inquiry later found much of the evidence was suspect, especially the evidence given by such eminent forensic experts as the British scientist, Professor James Cameron, at one time a consultant to Scotland Yard, and she was freed.

But what attracted Sheila to the movie was that the role of Lindy was to be played by Meryl Streep. 'It was only a little part but at the time I would have killed to do it, just to be able to say I worked with Meryl Streep,' said Sheila.

*Sheila Kennelly and Frank Lloyd who play Floss and Neville McPhee. Sheila turned down the chance to act alongside Meryl Streep to appear in 'Home and Away' ...*

Instead, she chose 'Home and Away'. Later she was to look back on her decision and wonder if she had done the right thing. 'The trouble was, the film schedule would have fallen into the first week's shoot of "Home and Away",' she said. 'It's nice to think I was almost in *Evil Angels*. It would have been nice to be splashed all over the world's cinemas.' And splashed is the right description. In The United States, *Evil Angels,* retitled *A Cry in the Dark,* opened to huge critical acclaim, not only for Meryl Streep but for her co-star, Sam Neill, who plays Michael Chamberlain.

So for Sheila it was 'Home and Away'. She took on the role of Floss McPhee, her screen husband, Neville McPhee, played by veteran actor, Frank Lloyd. The producers of the soap describe Floss and Neville as 'residents of the Summer Bay caravan park – a pensioner couple who have retired from their itinerant life on the carnival circuit. They've been together thirty-five years and are still in love. Floss is naturally gregarious, involved in all the social activities of the community. Where Neville tends to be stingy, she's open handed with her money and is always in strife with Neville because of it. To people who don't know them, it seems as if they are always bickering, but they both thoroughly enjoy their arguments. In their own way, they are devoted to one another.'

Sheila signed for 'Home and Away' with her eyes wide open. She knew the soapie business like the back of her hand, having spent four-and-a-half years in the infamous 'Number 96'. 'I'm one of the few who kept my clothes on,' she said.

Until 'Number 96' she had performed mostly in theatres and music halls. Born in Sussex, she came to Australia with her parents, then trained at the Independent Theatre. Her career was less than spectacular until she became Norma Whittaker in 'Number 96'. Within weeks she could not walk along the street without being accosted by fans, could not go to supermarkets or restaurants without being questioned and asked to apply her autograph to bits of paper. It was the same with all the cast. They drew crowds wherever they went. For instance, Channel Ten, which screened 'Number 96' put the cast aboard a train for a fourteen-hour overnight journey from Sydney to Melbourne. Throughout the night the train stopped at small stations, sometimes no bigger than a shed and a sign, but no matter what the time was a crowd was there to see the cast. And when the train arrived at Melbourne at 8am so many fans turned up the only thing stopping a riot was several lines of burly coppers.

With the money she earned from acting Sheila bought a property in the Hunter Valley, about two hours' drive from Sydney, nothing large, a mere 140 acres of rough scrub land. She cleared the land, fenced it, ploughed it, topdressed it, sowed oats and got together a herd of breeding cows and a bull.

The bull gave her a lot of problems. At first he wouldn't do what was expected of him, that is, get among the cows. Sheila thought it might have had something to do with his name, which was Fairy. She gave him medicine to help him on his way. Then he became too friendly, wandering from the paddocks into the house and eating the fruit off the sideboard. Fairy also took to sleeping on the verandah.

Sheila got a new bull she called Angus. He was much more sprightly than Fairy. 'He's a right little raver who keeps doing the wrong thing and breaking into the wrong paddocks to serve the heifers,' she said. 'It's so hard to keep him out. He just lifts the gate off its hinges and pushes solidly until he gets through.'

She cheerfully admitted one of her problems as a farmer was she was too soft when it came to parting with her breeding cows. 'If I was sensible, I would sell them when they were nine years old. But I don't. I keep them.'

Her role in 'Home and Away' meant she had to leave the farm before 5am to be in Sydney for the day's shoot. It was hard work. Sometimes she was up all night when the cows were calving. On some mornings she would find the creek flowing through her property would be flooded after a heavy night's rain and there was nothing she could do but wade through the muddy, swirling water. She put up with droughts, invasions of wallabies that would eat her oat crop, broken fences, sick cows, all the little things that make farming in Australia about as easy as climbing Everest. 'But I love it,' she would tell anyone within earshot. 'You know, a lot of actors keep farms and use them as retreats. It's just such a total contrast to the business. Until I went there I had no idea the country could give a person so much. I would be quite happy to spend the rest of my days there – it's my Utopia.'

Even though she was working long hours, Sheila was quite happy on 'Home and Away'. The soap was doing nicely. But there were some warning signs that a veteran actress like Sheila Kennelly could read. For instance, the carnival side of her character wasn't pursued. There was more emphasis on the younger members of the cast, to be expected in a soapie catering to kids up to eighteen or nineteen. But the world is not populated entirely by young people, as much as the media tries to pretend otherwise, and Sheila noted such things and wondered.

One of the penalties of working in soaps is that characters can easily be written out. They might be here today and gone tomorrow, a rooster one moment, a feather duster the next. American film director Carl Reiner recalled the days when he worked in radio soaps and noted the eagerness of actors to get to the network copying department for the next batch of scripts. Reiner thought this showed admirable keeness for their work until he discovered the actors were anxious to see if in the next few episodes they developed a cough. A cough in the script was a sign the character was developing consumption further along the road and was therefore being written out.

Soap contracts are written in a way that allows actors to be removed at short notice. Robert C. Allen, an American expert on television in general, and soaps in particular, explains it this way: 'An actor is under contract to a soap for a period of a year or more, during which time he/she is obligated to appear. Built into each contract, however, are thirteen or twenty-six week renewal periods at the end of which the actor's contract can be terminated by the production company. If viewer response to a new character fails to come up to expectations or if a plot-line falters, the storyline, character and actor can be disposed of quickly and economically. Within this system of labour relations lies a fundamental difference between soaps and prime-time shows … soaps are not star-oriented … the multiplot and multicharacter of the soaps puts power in the hands of the production company rather than the actors.'

Sheila knew the truth of these statements. When she was with 'Number 96', the producers, after watching the ratings slump, decided drastic measures were called for. They wrote a bomb explosion into the script. Four of its leading characters were written off in one noisy moment and Sheila's character was badly injured.

'Home and Away' had been running ten months when she was told her contract would not be renewed. Floss and Neville McPhee would depart for some other caravan park, either in this world or the next.

She was philosophical about it, even though she had given up her chance to act in a movie with Meryl Streep. '"Home and Away" has a huge following of very young people, so the writers and all concerned have to cater for them,' she said. 'Soaps are like repertory theatre – huge training grounds for young actors. Soaps offer a wonderful opportunity for them to develop their craft. I've been there and done that. But I'll always have plenty to do. And the farm is my first love.'

But they couldn't keep her down on the farm for long. Within weeks of learning she was to be written out Sheila was working on the pilot of another proposed soap, 'Somerset Street', about the lifestyles of workers, trendies and oldtimers in a suburban street. Its producer, Harry Michaels, hoped it would become Sydney's answer to Melbourne's 'Neighbours'.

Of course the exodus of Sheila Kennelly meant her screen husband, played by Frank Lloyd, had to go as well. There is little mercy in soaps. When it comes to dropping actors, soap producers sometimes show they have not drunk deeply of the milk of human kindness. But then they have to be ruthless because a soap cannot be allowed to bog down, not even for a night. There was so little mercy in Frank's case that he discovered he was about to be axed by reading it in a television magazine. 'We didn't think that was very nice of those concerned at all,' he said with classic understatement.

An actor of wide experience who has been in show business for more than forty years, Frank, sixty, worked in English pantomime, in Paris, Rome, where he dubbed films into English, Canada, starred as 'The Drunkard' on the New York stage and in the 1970s went to Moscow as a guest of the Ministry of Culture. He is an actor of the old school, well-rounded, capable of playing any part from dramatic roles to a song-and-dance man.

When he got the role of Neville McPhee in 'Home and Away', he was more than a little pleased. For one thing, he was a keen body surfer and Summer Bay was a place where the surf broke ceaselessly. He was working with Sheila Kennelly, who he described as 'an absolutely marvellous lady and a superb actress. We hit it off right from the word go and had some wonderful times.'

And he wasn't at odds with his character. He had a soft spot for the old trouper who had retired to a caravan nestled among the shrubbery of Summer Bay. 'Neville McPhee was decent, friendly, good living and someone who helped everybody else. I liked him very much.'

But into his life came a word often tossed about in television circles when producers can't think of any other reason for doing what they are about to do.

'It was all to do with demographics,' Frank said, mentioning the dreaded word. 'Apparently, according to television ratings, our characters were too old and not exciting enough for the viewers. We were told that a survey showed that rating figures were not as high when the oldies were on as they were when the kids were involved in the storylines. So that was that.'

Another original not to last the distance was Helena Bozich. Her removal from the show was unexpected because her character, Lynn Davenport, sounded interesting, at least on paper. According to the writers, Lynn,

*Frank Lloyd playing the bugle on Anzac Day. He enjoyed playing Neville McPhee – and enjoyed surfing at Summer Bay. But he was philosophical about his character being axed from the series*

thirteen, was 'the youngest of seven kids born to a family whose father is a manual worker, pulling in a poverty line salary. ... The tension in the family became intolerable for the sensitive young girl. Constant arguments made her decide anywhere was better than home. She ran away, to be found by the police, hungry and miserable in a storm-water drain. When she was brought home she had the living daylights beaten out of her. Life became even more intolerable. She ran away again four months later, only to be returned home. On the fifth runaway attempt, when she nearly lost her life, the welfare department intervened. They suggested to her parents they take the girl off their hands. ... At the age of ten, Lynn was put in a home where she pined. The institutionalised atmosphere oppressed her and once again she ran away. Two years after her coming to the home, the authorities in desperation decided to give her a go in a foster home. As Tom and Pippa were admired for their work with the difficult Frank and Carly, the department asked them to see what they could do with Lynn.'

Helena had been involved with acting since the age of eight when she joined the Australian Theatre for Young People, winning a scholarship with the company when she was thirteen. 'That's when I decided it was a lot of fun and wanted to keep going with it,' she said.

Settling into her role in 'Home and Away' she became the envy of friends who several times a week rang her home in the Sydney suburb of Kensington, with the warning: 'You're not allowed to get a big head ... and don't forget us.'

She didn't have time to forget them. Just as the news was announced that 'Home and Away' had been sold to Britain, possibly to rival 'Neighbours', she was called into head office and told her character was being 'rested', a word with a much gentler touch than 'axed'. Alan Bateman said that because of the size of the cast 'some of the characters get lost and don't appear on the screen for some time'.

Helena had learned that if she wanted a job with a secure future she should have become a computer operator or a secretary or a teacher, anything but show business.

She had learned the lesson at the age of fourteen.

# 12

## Looking Back on Success

As 'Home and Away' became accepted and kids started to annoy their parents by demanding the family television set be switched to the soap and not to the news, the Seven Network and the producers worked on ways to keep it in front of the public. Competitions were run in newspapers, including one that boasted the winner could have a family reunion anywhere in the world.

Special episodes were highlighted by intensive publicity campaigns, one of the most successful a storyline on wife-bashing. It was screened at a time when Australians were astonished to read in a government report that one in five people thought it all right for husbands to thump wives.

Liddy Clark, who played the victim, was appalled. 'I found playing the character a very frightening experience,' she said. 'It was very interesting because I had never played a victim before and the experience was something I would not like to have to repeat. It is important to note my character was beaten as a result of her husband drinking to excess, which I believe is one of the main causes of domestic violence. Everybody today keeps talking of the terrible effects of marijuana on society, yet alcohol and tobacco are still readily available.'

Of course, Summer Bay could not survive with only the original

*Liddy Clark (in apron) makes a guest appearance as a battered wife. (Left to right: Jeff Truman, Rob Baxter and Catherine McCall Jones)*

*No stranger to appearing on television with very few clothes on,*
*Greg Benson (who plays Matt the Surfie) made his first hit in a*
*Levi jeans advertisement*

characters inhabiting the place. It would seem as deserted as a church on a hot Sunday. Or a ghost town. There had to be visitors and one was Matt the Surfie.

Matt was played by Greg Benson who, at the age of twenty, reached a certain fame by removing his jeans in public. He was not arrested. The disrobing was for a Levi jeans commercial and showed Greg dropping his pants in a laundromat to display a fine pair of boxer shorts. Such is the power of television, even when it is showing commercials, he was credited with causing a revival in boxer shorts, a form of apparel he won't wear himself. 'The advertisement did a lot for me,' he said. 'I don't think I would be doing "Home and Away" if it wasn't for that.'

Greg lives in a kind of Summer Bay himself, a spot on the New South Wales Central Coast about an hour's drive north of Sydney, where the Pacific rolls mightily on to clean sand. He drove to work to play Matt the Surfie instead of taking the train because trains can have unexpected hazards for good-looking young men who have removed their pants on television. 'If you get on a train with a heap of teenage girls on board, it's a problem,' he said.

Darius Perkins was another arrival to Summer Bay, playing a character he described as 'fascinating. On the surface he comes across as Mr Nice Guy but underneath he's quite mixed up. He's a psychotic sociopath and very interesting to play.'

His character seems a world away from Scott Robinson, of 'Neighbours'. Darius played Scott for nine months before the role was taken over by Jason Donovan, who has gone on to become one of the world's great teenage idols. 'I blew it – it's that simple,' he said after he was replaced by Jason. 'I was too young and inexperienced to handle it. I was like a restrained monster.'

When 'Home and Away' was cast, the producers looked carefully at Darius for the leading role of Frank Morgan, which finally went to Alex Papps. 'He's a very talented young man,' said producer John Holmes. 'He did a fabulous screen test for me … I did look at him for the role of Frank in the early days.'

Now Darius can look back at what might have been, note what has happened and consider himself fortunate in some ways. 'I'm still glad I'm not with "Neighbours",' he said. 'I wouldn't want to be in Jason's shoes in a million years. I hope only the best for him but I wouldn't want to be him. I'd like to build a career slowly because that's the only way people grant you respect.'

Perhaps the biggest coup for 'Home and Away' was having rock singer John Farnham appear in two episodes. Farnham is a national hero in Australia, revered not only because of his singing successes with The Little River Band and as a solo artist but because he happens to be a nice guy. In 1988 he was made Australian of the Year.

And now here he was in Summer Bay. The reason for his visit was that he had done a multi-million dollar deal with Christopher Skase, head of the Seven Network. They owned Farnham for two years, although the popular belief was his contract would involve only television specials and rock concerts. The reasoning around Seven, however, is that if you pay millions to have exclusive rights to an entertainer, it would be foolish in the extreme not to use him in every possible way.

'It's not something I would have chosen to do, but now that it's happened I'm quite happy about it,' he said after his first soap experience.

*Top Australian singer and 1988's Australian of the Year, John
Farnham made a guest appearance on the series when he visited
Sally (Kate Ritchie) in her sickbed*

Farnham came to Summer Bay because of Sally Keating, played by
Kate Ritchie, the baby in the Fletcher household. Sally is an important
part of the Summer Bay scene. Said her biography, 'Sally was just three
when she lost her parents in a boating accident. She went to live with her
grandmother and her love helped Sally to adjust to the loss of her parents
and feel secure again. Then when she was five-and-a-half, Mrs Keating
was diagnosed as having Alzheimer's disease. ... One of her teachers
brought the situation to the attention of the welfare department who put
her in a home when they realised she wasn't being properly cared for. ...
Sally slept in the same dormitory as Lynn Davenport who quickly started
to mother Sally. When the authorities told Lynn they'd found a suitable
foster family for her, she refused to leave the home without Sally. Tom
and Pippa volunteered to take them both. On the surface she appears to
be a normal eight-year-old. But scratch the surface and you'll find a little
girl who can't make herself believe that Tom and Pippa are there for
good.'

The storyline involving John Farnham had Kate winning two tickets
to one of the singer's concerts. But because of chicken pox she could not
attend. Hearing of her grevious affliction, Farnham went to her bedside in
Summer Bay. Would Farnham be so philanthropic in real life? 'Yeah,' he

replied without hesitation when asked at the time. 'It's difficult sometimes. I can't do it all but I do as much as I can. The demands on my time are very heavy at the moment, so I can't visit everyone who's sick and who would like me to visit. I'd like to but I just can't. I do what I can when I do it. Ultimately, all it takes is a little bit of energy … but I have to draw the line sometimes because I have to live my life as well.'

Farnham is no stranger to acting. In 1977 he starred as an up-and-coming pop star in a half-hour comedy series called 'Bobby Dazzler'. But Farnham wasn't as big in those days, furthermore the series was a little short on comedy. It was axed after a few months. He also hosted a game show called 'Opportunity Knocks'. It was axed as well.

Admitting that television was not his favourite medium, he said he only felt comfortable when singing. 'I've tried to be natural in "Home and Away" and it was quite an interesting experience. I'm sure everyone has been through this since the advent of the home video recorder: when you take photographs of your kids, your grandma, your mum and dad, your aunt and uncle or yourself, and somebody always says, "just be natural". That's the second hardest thing to do in front of a camera. When you first hear your voice on a tape recorder there's a squirm factor. It's the same thing when you see yourself on television. I can't watch. I can listen, but I can't watch.'

Meeting Farnham, tagged Whispering Jack by his fans and the media, didn't bother Kate Ritchie. 'He's really nice,' she said. 'He doesn't think he's anything special because he's famous. He's not big-headed.'

The same can be said for Kate, nine, who has been in a number of commercials and played the child lead in the mini-series, 'Cyclone Tracy'. Someone once told her she was a star. She shook her head firmly. 'Oh, I hardly think I'm a star. I'm only nine years old. Don't you have to be older than that?'

Like many children she has a way of putting life into perspective. Where other actors may have looked back on 1988 as the year they found fame, if not fortune, on 'Home and Away' , the year the soap was sold to Britain, Kate saw things differently.

She was asked what was the best thing that happened to her during the year.

'Our cat Socksie had seven little kittens,' she said proudly.